THE
GOD
WE NEVER KNEW

EMPOWERING **WOMEN** WITH
THE **TRUTH** OF
WHO THEY ARE

TRISHA BIESINGER

THE GOD WE NEVER KNEW
EMPOWERING **WOMEN** WITH THE **TRUTH** OF WHO THEY ARE
Copyright © 2024 by Trisha Biesinger

To request permissions, contact the publisher at
publish@joapublishing.com.

Hardcover ISBN: 978-1-961098-78-7
Paperback ISBN: 978-1-961098-77-0
eBook ISBN: 978-1-961098-79-4
Printed in the USA.

Joan of Arc Publishing
Meridian, ID 83646
www.joapublishing.com

DEDICATION

To my grandmothers—
Who rebuilt their lives with unwavering grace,
Who loved fiercely through broken hearts,
Who created beauty from emptiness—
Your courage flows through my veins.

To all the women who walked before me—
Those left, abused, or told there were not enough,
The mothers who work tirelessly,
Feeling unseen and undervalued,
Yet show up in love every day—
I dedicate this book to you.

And to my clients—
The women I have sat with through your pain—
May these words bring you hope, renewed faith,
And an unshakable resolve that you are divine,
More worthy than you can comprehend,
And more valuable than the world can afford.

These words were written for you.
You are more than enough.
You deserve to be seen, to be heard,
And to be loved exactly as you are.

I USED TO PRAY TO PLEASE.

NOW I PRAY TO RECEIVE.

-Trisha

TABLE OF CONTENTS

PREFACE

It's 10 p.m. and you're standing in your kitchen—that familiar battlefield of crusty dishes and half-eaten snacks. Your hair hasn't seen shampoo in days, and your "workout clothes" have witnessed more cleaning than actual workouts. The toddler tornado that swept through your house today has finally settled, leaving behind a trail of crumbs, missing shoes, and your last thread of patience.

To escape the overwhelm of your life for a moment, you begin scrolling.

There's Sarah from high school, somehow defying physics in her unwrinkled, white linen dress, laughing carelessly on a beach you can't pronounce. Her children—who surely can't be real children—are all smiles in their matching outfits, building Instagram-worthy sandcastles while her husband gazes lovingly from afar. And there you are, wearing yesterday's t-shirt decorated with mysterious stains (is that peanut butter or . . . something else?), wondering how your life ended up so far from the highlight reel that's playing out on your screen.

Your thumb hovers over the like button—that familiar dance of obligation and envy—while that voice inside whispers what it always does: "Everyone else has figured it out, everyone but me."

We've all lived this moment—that late-night spiral when our beautiful mess of reality crashes into the carefully curated façades we're bombarded with daily; the constant feeling that we're somehow falling behind, missing the mark, or failing at this whole life thing. But what if I told you that Sarah from high school spent forty-five minutes positioning her "candid" beach photo? That her perfect children were bribed with ice cream and promises of screen time? That behind her radiant smile was a woman just as lonely, just as uncertain, just as desperate to feel "enough" as you?

What if I told you that behind every filtered photo and carefully crafted caption lies a story just as complicated, just as imperfect, just as beautifully human as yours? That the woman who seems to have it all together is lying awake at night, wrestling with the same doubts, fears, and heartbreaks you do?

If you've ever felt your worth dissolve in the glow of someone else's life, if you've exhausted yourself trying to earn love that should be freely given, if you've whispered prayers into your pillow wondering why you never seem to be enough—

This book is for you.

It's for those nights you lie awake replaying your mistakes, fearing you're doing it all wrong. For the moments you leave social events feeling small, worried you said too much or too little, often feeling overwhelmed by the thought that no one likes you.

It's for the days the scale feels like a judge and your worth seems tied to a number, when clothes don't fit and leave you in tears as you compare yourself to those who appear effortlessly beautiful.

It's for the times you carry the weight of others' emotions, blaming yourself for their unhappiness, bending over backward to meet expectations, only to see them disappointed and frustrated with you time and time again.

2

It's for mothers who watch others living adventurous lives online as they change another diaper, wear the same clothes from the day before, and clean messes they didn't make for the hundredth time—drowning in work that often goes unnoticed and unappreciated.

It's for women who are submerged in the depths of motherhood—waiting to be desired, noticed, appreciated, and supported—longing for dreams they once held but now feel too exhausted to chase.

It's for the moments you doubt your worth in every relationship, especially the one with God, feeling like unconditional love is always out of reach.

This message is for every woman who stands in the shadow of self-doubt, questioning if she'll ever truly be enough or find an inner peace that lasts beyond the moment.

This book is more than just words on a page. It's a passionate reminder of your divine nature, your innate worth, and the powerful truth that you are so much more than the roles you play or the judgments you face. This book invites you to remember the miracle of who you are, to rise with confidence and acknowledge that you are more than enough **exactly as you are.**

If any of these words resonate with you, then know that you're not alone.

This book is for you.

And this book was written for me. You see, I *never* imagined myself as an author; I never dreamed of writing a book. I never felt good enough, smart enough, or like I had whatever it takes to be a writer. I lived to please other people, and thought everyone's love for me was tied to what I did for them.

I have been bold and adventurous in many aspects of life, often the first to try new things and take risks, a wild extrovert who loved gathering people together. Yet, putting my deepest thoughts into words and sharing them with the world feels incredibly terrifying.

Of all the brave things I've done in my life, writing a book feels like the bravest of all. Allowing others to read my words and understand my thoughts has pushed me to overcome some of my deepest fears of being seen.

And honestly, a part of me wants to keep this book to myself, fearing it's not for everyone, thinking of all the people who might not agree with what I have to say, but I refuse to live in fear, so here I am, jumping into the unknown to bring you these words in the most miraculous way.

THE JOURNEY OF
WRITING THIS BOOK

I never thought I would be here, writing these words to you. I think it is important that you know how this book came to be, so you can understand the miracle of these pages. Most of my life I've been told I was a great listener, and I do love to listen, but mostly because I was afraid to speak because when I did share my thoughts or insights, they were not always warmly received by those closest to me. So I became a great listener because it felt safe. As long as I wasn't the one talking, there was nothing to worry about. If someone asked about me, I would often find a way to turn the conversation back to them, back to safety. I also realized that if I listened to people talk about themselves, they seemed to like me more. It was so strange because I usually didn't share much about myself. At a young age, I came up with the idea that people didn't need to like me, **they needed to like themselves**. So I got really good at agreeing, people-pleasing, listening, and giving people what I believed they wanted.

Writing nearly 200 pages filled with my passionate thoughts, ideas, and purpose is one of the most daunting things I've ever done. It's not hard to write these thoughts on empty pages—that's the easy part—it's knowing that someone else will read them, and being deeply known has never felt safe for me. I've always preferred to keep my most profound thoughts and feelings to myself, choosing instead to listen as others share theirs.

But this message isn't mine to keep. This book isn't filled with just my thoughts. This book is God's, and as much as I have wrestled with it, resisted it, and tried to not finish it, I know it isn't about me. It came through me for you. And so with all the courage I can muster, I invite you in. I invite you to sit with these words knowing the miraculous way they landed here on these pages.

For you.
For me.
From God.

A God that I think differently about after writing this book. As you read, I hope you will meet God in a new way, as I have.

I wrote this book in a very unique way. I went on an author adventure with my publisher and book medium, Keira Brinton. She inspires and helps people to write their most important messages *with God*. She takes authors to amazing locations and uses a process that calms their nervous systems, ignites their creativity, collapses time, and centers them in their hearts, allowing them to connect with God and bring forth powerful messages that change the world.

I never considered writing a book until I saw how Keira helps others do it. Her Instagram stories captured my attention as she showed authors embarking on adventures to write entire books in just five days! It seemed both unbelievable and magical. And if you know me, you know I LOVE adventure, stepping outside the norm, and trying new things, especially doing what seems impossible.

I started to wonder if I could write a book in this way—in just five days. The thought seemed fun and exciting, but then doubt would rush in and tell me that I couldn't. I'm not a writer, and I worried God wouldn't help *me* write a book. I thought maybe it only worked for other people because they were more capable, and God could work through them, but not me.

And to be honest, I didn't even know what I wanted to write about!

I just felt so drawn to this experience, and I couldn't shake it, though I tried for months.

One day I commented on one of Keira's Instagram posts about her latest author adventure. I said, "I have a book to write." She messaged me back a few hours later and said, "If you have a message to share, let's get that book out into the world." I felt my heart drop to my toes. I was nervous yet excited. To feel called to something but not know why, or what the message was supposed to be, felt so weird, and made it so easy to doubt.

As I sat with Keira on Zoom talking about what this book adventure entailed, I asked her, "What if God doesn't speak to me? What if I get there and I'm left to write this book by myself without God? What if I just sit there staring at blank pages with no inspiration and leave without a book?" She looked me straight in the eyes and said, "That will not happen. How many people are going to the mountains to meet God and receive a message to change the world? If you go, God will speak to you."

I wanted to believe her words, but I was so scared. I have believed in God all my life, but had never done something like this. Relying on a miracle, I signed up, paid, and hoped God would give me a full book in a matter of days. I didn't know if God worked like that, or if I deserved such a thing. But I decided to go. There are only a few times I've ever faced this much self-doubt in my life. To invest the time and money and hope that God would help me do what seemed impossible to my mind, to my self-beliefs, to what I thought was possible *for me*, was so scary. I had to believe in something I had *no experience in.*

In the months leading up to the adventure, I felt more fear than belief. I wanted to change my mind many times. I felt so much resistance, but I had to try—I wanted to see if God would show up for me—knowing that I felt called to share a message. It burned inside my soul. So, I clung to that small drop of belief for three months, hoping it would be enough.

I feared every day that I would get there and God would be *silent.*

But I had to know. I couldn't shake it. I knew I was supposed to write a book, and this was the way I was supposed to do it.

As the adventure got closer, my brain came up with all kinds of thoughts and evidence that this wouldn't work for me: reminding me how I never loved reading books growing up, and how it's been so long since I've written anything; reminding me that I am currently a part of a book club, and I haven't read any of the books!

But as you will soon find out, those thoughts were based on *who I thought I was*—the thoughts my brain used to keep me safe, small, and quiet, not wanting to speak for fear of rejection.

But I choose to create my life despite the thoughts that run through my mind.

So I didn't listen to the doubt.

Instead, I did what I KNEW I was here to do.

Which was to write this book. To share what I believe so passionately. To speak and allow others to hear it.

This book is proof that you can do anything.

This book is here to help YOU live the life you are destined to live, no matter what current thoughts you have about yourself, no matter the limits of your mind, or what you have been told.

This book is a miracle.

As are you.

Section 1

DEFINING SELF—SHAPING YOUR IDENTITY THROUGH THOUGHTS AND BELIEFS

THE MIRACLE OF YOUR EXISTENCE: PERFECTLY PLACED IN THE UNIVERSE. AMID LIFE'S CHALLENGES, REMEMBER THE WONDER AND IMPROBABILITY OF SIMPLY BEING HERE.

Chapter 1

SHE THROWS LIKE A BOY

I grew up as the youngest of four, just under twin brothers who often used me as a punching bag, a prop in their magic shows—locking me in boxes—and teasing me relentlessly. It was a bit like the *Hunger Games* at times, and I had to be quick, strong, and resourceful to navigate life as the baby sister. I was born brave and fearless, with a love for adventure and a healthy dose of adrenaline!

I was fiercely determined, never wanting to be limited by anything, especially not because I was a girl. As I grew up, I wanted every right and opportunity the boys had. Yet, I often heard boys around me using anything feminine as an insult to put each other down. They would often yell phrases like these at each other:

"You throw like a girl."
"You are acting like a girl."
"Don't be an emotional girl."
"Girls get picked last."
"Girls can't play sports."
"Girls can't throw a football."
"Girls are weak."
"You're such a girl."

Whether I was in class or on the playground, those words lingered in my mind. My identity was often used as a way to mock a boy perceived as weak or unable to do something remarkable.

At such a young age I got the message that I wasn't enough *just because I was a girl*. I was the weaker of the sexes: too sensitive, too emotional, incapable, and less than the boys.

This stung every time I heard it. Every time I was on the playground and standing with a group of kids as team captains picked people to be on their team for baseball, soccer, football, basketball—anything—all the boys were picked first, and then the captains just casually picked the girls because they had to. It never seemed like girls were important additions to the team.

This lit a fire in my little girl heart, and I was determined to prove that I was every bit as strong and capable as the boys at anything!

I would stand there patiently waiting, only to be one of the last picked for every sport. Energy would fill my body, like hot fire through my veins, as I would think to myself, *You think we are weak? Oh, you just wait!* And game after game my team would win. I was often the one who scored the winning touchdown or kicked the last goal. I was a fierce competitor and was determined to prove that girls were as capable as boys.

I remember when I was in eighth grade, every day in one of my classes the boys would arm wrestle to prove who was strongest and to gain respect and attention from the girls. I would look from across the room and think, *I bet I can beat them.* Maybe this was my chance after years of being told that girls are weaker. This was my moment to prove them all wrong. This was my time to make them know that we were just as strong, or maybe stronger.

One day, I walked up to the big round table full of loud boys who were arm wrestling and said, "I wanna try." They all paused, looked at me in shock, and laughed. "You want to arm wrestle us?" they asked. I said, "Yes, I do!" Their faces turned red as they looked around to see who wanted to beat me. One boy said, "OK, let's do this." "It's on!" I said.

There I was, one of the smallest, shortest girls with the softest voice and the bravest heart, sitting across the table from one of the loudest, proudest boys in the class. All the other boys stood in a circle around us mocking him, saying, "Don't get beat by a girl!" And that was just the fuel I needed. I sat up tall, we locked hands, and he smirked at me with such confidence. "Go!" the boys shouted, and I put in all the strength and all the pain that my little self had carried for years being told I was less than, weak, and incapable. I felt more determined than ever. I tightened my grip, looked him square in the eye, and took his arm down to the table with such force that I left a wave of shock throughout the whole classroom. All I heard was a gasp, and then silence as I stood up and said, "Girls are strong too." And I walked away.

For the next few weeks, I was known as the girl that could beat the boys in arm wrestling and sports. Every day in the same class someone was voted to challenge me to an arm wrestle. And nine times out of ten, I would win. And each time, the boys got more nervous and more embarrassed to lose.

All I wanted was to give us girls the recognition and respect we deserved. But after every game and every arm wrestle, you know what I heard?

"Woah, she actually knows how to play!"
"She arm wrestles like a boy!"
"She throws like a boy!"
"She looks like a girl but acts like a boy!"

Over time family members, friends, and kids at school started calling me a tomboy. I couldn't be a regular girl and play sports like that. I couldn't be the MVP of the team, I couldn't kick the winning goal or hit the baseball that far if I was *just* a girl. I must have been part boy, and my name must be Tom instead of Trisha.

To this day, every time I throw a football, win at Ping-pong, swing a bat, snowboard, or do anything adventurous, I still hear the gasps as people still say things like, "You throw like a boy." I'm a grown woman who has been strong, capable, smart, and brave my whole life, and am now a mother who created three humans through the most exquisite pain a human can endure.

And If I throw a ball, I'm recognized for my strength. I'm cheered for doing the impossible. The shock of what I can do rings through the air.

But never as I carry a child in my womb, never as I clean the whole house while I have the stomach flu, never as I chase a rogue child through the grocery store, or go without breakfast, lunch, and dinner because I'm too busy taking care of everyone else. Never as I wake up ten times a night with young babies, or sit on a tailbone broken from childbirth.

That's just what moms do. We barely notice it or get praise for it.

All this time that I was trying to prove I was as strong and capable as the boys, I never realized that my strength as a girl, and as a woman, far exceeded throwing a ball or winning an arm wrestle. My strength is so vast that it can't be measured on the football field. It can't be comprehended by others, so they've never acknowledged it.

As a woman, if you ever heard the same things I did growing up . . . get ready to see yourself in a whole new light as you read these pages!

Chapter 2

THE TIME I LOST GOD

About six years ago, I tragically lost a cousin that was my age and in my stage of life: a new mom with two little kids. She was so radiant, a woman full of light and love. I often saw her pictures on Instagram as she played with her girls and enjoyed motherhood. I felt connected to her because I was a new mom raising babies as well. Even though we didn't see each other often and weren't very close, I felt connected to her as we shared this phase of life. She was loved by all who knew her, and I admired who she was.

When she was placed on life support, I remember falling to my knees in prayer, with every ounce of belief that if I prayed to the God I had always relied on and trusted in, my cousin would receive a miracle. I was convinced that if I prayed with all the faith I had, she would fully recover and live to raise her babies.

I don't think I had ever prayed that hard in my life, desperate for a life to remain. And I know I'm not the only one that has said *this* prayer, tears streaming down, stomach in knots, trying to say the right words, begging for a miracle.

I couldn't imagine God not answering this prayer. It wasn't only my prayer but the prayer of so many others as well. I thought if I had faith, belief, and said a powerful prayer, **she would live**. While she was in the hospital I prayed multiple times a day trying to move heaven, trying to convince God this was the right miracle to give, asking, begging, selling, whatever I could think of. I feared that if this tragedy could happen to her, it could happen to me too. If God could allow her children to live without their mother, He could allow mine to live without me.

I wanted her to wake up and return to her family and her beautiful life that I admired, to be there for her young babies, to live a full life with her husband who deeply loved her.

Despite all the prayers, faith, and wanting, my prayers weren't answered.

My cousin passed away.

And I was in shock.

Disbelief.

How could this happen to a young mom? How could this happen to her husband and her little girls? How could God NOT answer *this* prayer?

This event changed me.

And no one knew.

I didn't talk about it. But slowly, over time, I went from trusting God, believing in God, praying daily to God . . .

to questioning God.

My belief was slowly turning into doubt, and my faith into fear.

My love for God turned into bitterness and resentment.

He was a God that no longer felt safe.

I kept praying with my family before meals and with my children before bed, but I didn't feel that same belief in prayer. I said the words, but didn't feel the answers. I didn't even notice this was happening until years later when my own personal prayers became less frequent, and then I avoided prayers completely.

I just didn't see the point in them anymore.

I figured no matter what I asked for, prayed for, God was going to do what He wanted anyway.

I write this because I know I am not the only one who has experienced an unanswered prayer, a devastating loss, immense grief, or heartbreaking disappointment. And as much as I want to keep this experience to myself and go on pretending I've never lost faith and never doubted, that would be a lie. I no longer want to believe that it's wrong to doubt. Doubt can open us up to powerful questions and eventually lead us to a deeper belief and understanding.

For a long time I felt shame that I had no desire to pray. Prayer had been a daily practice my whole life, and now I felt like I couldn't even force myself to do it. I didn't want to talk to a God that didn't listen when it mattered most. I didn't want to believe in something that I couldn't trust. I felt hurt and didn't want to keep asking God for help when I wasn't sure if or when He would show up.

I decided to just rely on myself; it seemed safer. If I could trust me and be there for me, maybe I didn't need God. And I didn't think God needed me either.

I like to focus on what I can control, and I knew I couldn't control God.

I wanted to believe, but I was afraid.

I knew I needed a way back, and I believe that is why God led me here to Mill Valley, California on a book adventure with a woman named Keira who believes so fiercely in God and constantly reminds people that **if you ask, you shall receive**. I wanted to believe this again too.

I woke up the first morning of the book adventure, unsure if God would show up. Here I was hoping to do the impossible with a God I was now scared of. I walked out to the front yard, into a garden of flowers, sat on a lounge chair in the sun, closed my eyes, and simply asked God to write through me as I was staring at blank pages.

And God showed up

despite my doubts, despite my fear, in all my imperfect faith.

God wasn't silent,

not for one minute.

As I opened my computer to write this book with only one drop of belief, God poured out these words and a message of love and hope like I have never heard before—words my mind couldn't have written on its own, a message so powerful, so beautiful even I can't believe I wrote it.

These words are holy, not because I am holy, for they are not mine.

These words brought me back to God. Not the God I thought I knew before but a whole new God.

These words healed me, and I hope they heal you too.

Chapter 3

THE MIRACLE
OF YOUR CREATION

It is a complete miracle that you were born, carried in a womb, and built piece by piece by a mother—every cell, intricate organ and vein, all the bones perfectly placed to give you life, a heart that beats fast or slow depending on what you need, lungs that breathe without conscious thought. Everything works together like a beautiful symphony to keep you alive, so you can exist on this planet with the perfect amount of air to breathe, water to drink, and gravity to hold you on this earth that is the perfect distance from the sun and moon to give you both life and rest.

It all works for *you* and gives you everything you need to live, to be.

Why?

Why you?

Why here?

Why now?

It all works so magically, so seamlessly, second by second so you can be here right *now*, in a way and for a reason no one comprehends. How is it that the earth has exactly what our bodies need, and no matter how much food or water we consume, there's always more? It replenishes itself over and over. The trees breathe in what we don't need and out what we do, cleaning the air, giving us more oxygen. The oceans are so vast and deep we can't explore it all. The seasons change, giving us time to play in the sun and time to heal in the dark, seeming to know just what we need. And if any of it is off by even the slightest bit, we cease to exist. If gravity isn't exactly perfect, there is no life.

Some think this is all random and that it must have happened by accident. The earth, sun and moon, mountains, oceans, and stars—and all of us—just happened because a few things bumped together in the sky. And maybe it is all random, a perfect accident. Or maybe it was created with purpose and intention—organized and planned—every piece designed in love, for life.

We cannot see inside a mother's womb and understand exactly how life is created. She creates life without thought, without conscious understanding of how it's done. She can't explain it in words, but as she sleeps, eats, showers, and goes about her day, somehow her body just knows how to create a life. The mind doesn't comprehend the how. She doesn't have to take a class, pass a test, and feel ready before she creates a human. She doesn't decide when the heart should beat or where the bones go. She doesn't have to think about it at all, just as we don't have to make the world turn, the sun rise, or the rain fall. We don't have to think about it *for it to be so*.

We don't know why or how it all works, it just does. And what if it's all *for* you and *for* me?

You came here unique, the only version of you in the world. No one is the same. No one is just like you.

It is all miraculous, and so are you.

Chapter 4

WHO YOU THOUGHT YOU NEEDED TO BE

At a young age you probably heard many voices telling you when you were right and when you were wrong, what to do, and who you "should be." You paid attention to what people liked and didn't like and adjusted accordingly. You soaked in the "shoulds" and tried to be all of it for everyone.

It was as if that was your purpose: to make people pleased, happy, and proud.

Maybe you heard you were "the shy one," or "too quiet."

Then from someone else, "You're too loud, hyper, or difficult."

Some words stung and didn't feel true, but you thought, *Maybe they know who I am better than I do.*

Some opinions of you felt good, like a warm blanket, and you wanted them to be true. And some hurt to the core. All optional, all observations. But to you, they seemed relevant and important to remember.

It can be so confusing growing up in a little body with a new brain, trying to find safety with who you are. Your brain's ultimate job is to keep you safe, so it pays attention to what others want you to be to ensure you aren't rejected or abandoned.

As you grew you tried to be what was accepted and wanted. But with each new person you were with it became more and more difficult. They all seemed to want different versions of you. Some needed you to be fun and entertaining while others wanted you to be calm and quiet—anything that made them more comfortable.

It can become so easy to be a people pleaser without even noticing it because your brain believes if people are pleased you will be safe and have a better chance at survival. The brain knows that surviving will be much more difficult if you are alone. So it goes to work trying to be what everyone wants.

It doesn't seem as important to the brain to learn and understand who you are, what you like and dislike, what you want to do or be. Doing what feels most authentic and comfortable to you doesn't seem like the priority because the brain knows you can't physically abandon yourself.

So it focuses on pleasing everyone else.

This can leave you feeling lost and confused about who you are. Sometimes it seems that people like you, and sometimes not. And no matter how many versions of you that you have created for everyone, you can't seem to please them all, leaving you exhausted.

I know because I've been there.

As a child, I was highly observant. Being the youngest in the family, I constantly watched my siblings, noticing what earned praise and what didn't as I tried to navigate this life with the least amount of pain or problems.

At a young age I thought I figured out the perfect recipe for an easy life. If I followed it, I wouldn't be alone or rejected, and I would be safe. Or so *I thought*.

It looked something like this:

- Listen without disagreeing.
- Like what they like.
- Validate their feelings.
- Don't burden them with your needs.
- Be happy, no matter what.
- Play dumb so they can feel smart.
- Don't have my own opinions.

Mix it and let settle for a nice, peaceful life!

This recipe seemed to work every time. I made a lot of friends and would often hear, "Everyone likes you." And it felt good to be liked! So I kept this pattern of pleasing. Over time I started to wonder if it really was *me* that people liked or if it was just easier for them to like *themselves* around me because I was focused on liking them and being what they wanted and needed. I wasn't even being me sometimes; I was just giving them a lot of space to be themselves. I had followed the recipe to be liked, only to realize no one really *knew* me, so being liked wasn't as fulfilling as I thought it would be.

If I could fade into the background and let them shine by agreeing with their thoughts, laughing at their jokes, and enjoying whatever they thought was fun, they would feel comfortable being themselves. They could hear themselves talk, they believed they were smart and funny, and often they would *tell me* it was me they liked, but I knew they didn't need to know me. They just needed to know themselves more.

I didn't consciously know I was doing this. It was a pattern my brain picked up to keep me safe—safe from judgment, rejection, and loss. It seemed more important that people like a surface version of me than to risk rejection after being authentic and truly known.

Although I was pretty good at pleasing people, *I* rarely felt pleased. But I didn't think it was important or even "good" to make sure I was pleased. This is the pattern people pleasers fall into, so worried and focused on not being abandoned by others that they don't notice all the ways they **abandon themselves**.

By trying to be liked by everyone, I had abandoned myself. I didn't speak up or voice my opinions. I didn't offer what I was passionate about. I didn't add my unique ideas that could have had a great impact. I didn't know that liking myself mattered. But if we don't like ourselves, we don't share what we were created to share.

If we don't see our value, we don't add the value we came here to add.

To all the people pleasers out there: continue to be kind, helpful, compassionate, and great listeners, but remember that you don't have to abandon yourself to be those things for others. You matter too. You didn't come here to please. You weren't created in such a miraculous way to just act like everyone else. You weren't given divine uniqueness just to follow the crowd.

If you live your life to please others, they may never be pleased and will most likely always want more, but I know for sure *you* won't be pleased with yourself. Your life is far too important to hide in fear of not being liked.

If people don't like you, it says more about them than it does about you. Breathe that in because it's true. When people don't like themselves, it is rare that they like others.

Learn to like you before you focus on who else likes you.

Because if you like you, you will show up vastly different in life and in relationships, and you will create a life you love. You will like more people because you like you first. And you will believe others like you too, even if they don't.

This is the secret the world never taught us.

Chapter 5

WHO I THOUGHT I WAS

When you don't know yourself, you are left wide open for the world to tell you who you are. Anyone's opinion can feel true, which leads to confusion, doubt, and never feeling enough.

Your beliefs about who you are impact every aspect of your life.

About a year ago, as my husband and I were driving to dinner, we were talking about our dreams and what we wanted to create in the coming year. He wanted to start a new business and share his music with the world.

As a life coach, I wanted to empower more women and transform relationships.

As I was talking, I said, "Maybe I should write a book."

And as I said those words, I felt a wave of doubt rush through my body. It felt as strange as if I'd said, "I should be an astronaut." It might not have felt weird for someone else to want to write a book, but for me, that thought contradicted the beliefs I had about myself— who I thought I was, what I thought I was good at and capable of. Beliefs run our lives. **They are the made up rules we live by**. So the idea of writing a book felt shocking because it didn't fit the beliefs of who I thought I was. I never considered myself an author, or even someone who liked reading books.

So I never dreamed of writing a book. I didn't think I wanted to.

I had spent most of my adult years studying psychology, human behavior, and how beliefs impact our lives. Nothing fascinated me more. I graduated with my undergrad in psychology and went on to The Life Coach School to better understand the behavior of the brain and how to help people better navigate this life.

I spent a lot of time learning how our thoughts turn into deep beliefs, ultimately impacting everything we do. This changed my life, and now I see it change the lives of all of my clients I coach. I wanted to share this as far and wide as I could. I thought writing a book would be the best way to share it. I knew this would be a book I myself needed years ago, and I wondered if others did too.

I didn't know the details of what, when, or how to go about writing and publishing a book.

I just let myself imagine this book while driving in the car, wondering how I would tell the world the things that saved me and what I wished I had learned far sooner.

As I was describing what I would write about, my husband got excited and said, "You totally should write that book! It would be amazing!"

And I was like, "Me?! Write a book?"

Immediately, I could see myself in second grade, only seven years old in a small trailer classroom, separate from the rest of the school.

I remember standing at the edge of my teacher's desk. I can still recall her name and the accent she spoke with.

I was so young, just learning how to read. It was new. But I thought I was good at it. I remember thinking I was catching on and reading so fast for my age. Every reading assignment seemed easy, and I felt proud of myself.

So when she called us up one by one to read a paragraph out loud, I wasn't nervous. I was excited to show her how good I was.

I marched up to her desk, and I started to read, so proud of each word I thought I got right.

When I was finished, she paused. She didn't smile or say, "Great job!" She simply said, "It seems like you might be behind, but don't worry I'll send you to the class where they can help you catch up. It's called *resource.*"

I immediately knew what that was. And I sank. All the excitement and energy left my body, like water draining from a bath, out through my toes.

I was embarrassed and felt frozen to the edge of her desk, wishing I could have done better, confused at why I'd thought I was an amazing reader just minutes before, hoping for a second chance to read a little faster, to get the words just right. I didn't want to tell my friends that I had to go to resource. I didn't want them to know I couldn't read.

All the thoughts and doubts filled my little seven-year-old mind.

> *Maybe I'm not as smart as I thought.*
>
> *I don't know how to read.*
>
> *I'm behind.*

Is something wrong with me?

Will I ever catch up?

She sent me to another trailer classroom on the opposite side of the playground.

I walked alone, embarrassed.

Ashamed, I opened the large, heavy, metal door. A man walked up to me and asked why I was there. I heard my little voice shake as I said, "I can't read."

He smiled, nodded, and showed me where to sit. He sat down next to me and asked me to start reading a book. Just twenty minutes earlier I was confident, but now I was nervous.

I started to read the book, not trusting myself to know if I was good or bad, getting it right or wrong, and as I finished I looked up and heard him say, "You are a fantastic reader. I don't know why your teacher sent you here."

I was so relieved! I did it! I knew I could read! He sent me back to my classroom, and as I walked back, I was confused. Who was right and who was wrong about me? Was my teacher right, and was I behind and slow? Or was he right, and was I fantastic?

I didn't know at seven years old that **I could just decide**, that each teacher had a different idea of what was good, but I could also have an opinion for myself and believe it.

Because I was still unsure, I was led to question myself, as most of us do. And like all brains, mine wanted to avoid the thing I didn't think I was good at.

Throughout school, I avoided reading books unless I had to. I convinced myself, *I just don't like reading*. And I dove into sports and anything else that didn't require much reading.

I remember doing a book report on *Harry Potter* when I was in eighth grade. I got an A on that book report, and never read the book! I had sat through twenty *Harry Potter* book reports from the students before me, so I simply repeated what they said.

Part of me felt guilty, and part of me felt resourceful! I can get an A on a book report from a book I didn't HAVE to read!

For my reading homework I would often turn TV shows on Closed Captioning, leaving the volume up, and "read" my favorite show to pass off my thirty minutes of reading for school.

Again, resourceful!

I didn't even realize I was avoiding reading, or recognize it was because of that one day in second grade when my teacher said I was behind.

This is why the thought of becoming an author felt so strange. Me, write a book after I had found so many creative ways to avoid reading most of my life? That's not who I am.

Or so I've always thought.

And here I am—someone who once thought she didn't read well enough, and therefore couldn't write words that others would want to read—writing to you now, writing my first book and doing it in just five days to show my seven-year-old self that I can, showing second-grade me that how fast I read in second grade never defined who I was or who I could become, proving to myself that I don't have to be perfect to create powerful work and that it's possible to write an entire book without having read many.

I'm writing this to you! You, who also once believed a painful thought about who you are; for you who have been told that you weren't good enough at something or for someone else; for those who thought you had to be perfect to create something valuable. I write to you to show you what is possible when you challenge the opinions and thoughts of others, and show you what can change by letting go of the limiting beliefs that you've carried for too long. To you I say loud and clear that **you are allowed to believe whatever you want about yourself without permission**.

And if you choose what to believe about yourself, you will create your own safety that no one can take away. Words won't hold as much meaning for you unless you want them to. People won't have power over how you feel about yourself unless you let them.

You get to decide it all, and I'll show you how.

Chapter 6

LOST IN THE WAVES
OF APPROVAL

We all start out small, innocent, and trusting. We don't know our identity, so we look for it in other people.

As we grow, we quickly notice how to receive praise:

- taking our first steps—*cheers from our parents;*
- sharing our favorite toy—*praise from others;*
- winning the game—*praise from our coaches;*
- being quiet and obedient—*praise from loved ones.*

We see the reactions in others from what we do and don't do, and we start to attach who we are to what we get praised for.

We look toward others as mirrors to see if we are good enough.

We notice others' expressions, mannerisms, tone, and words as important information to decide if we are worthy, valuable, and right.

We don't crave our own praise because we don't consider it important or necessary.

Because of this we often don't notice what we think of ourselves, and we hyper focus on what others think of us.

It's all that seems to matter.

And when it's all that matters, we live for it! And then we lose ourselves in an ocean of opinions, voices, judgments, doubts, assumptions, comments, criticisms, or even praise. We're tossed around by differing opinions of who we are, and those opinions contradict each other like crashing waves of confusion.

Sometimes we are up, and sometimes we are down, thrown around by the thoughts of others,

> *depending on them,*
> *needing their approval,*
> *desperate to be seen,*
> *starving for love and connection.*

Sometimes we want to stand out and be seen. We want to be loud and grab attention.

See me! Tell me I'm good, accepted, and wanted!

And other times we want to hide, shrink, blend in, and go unnoticed, ebbing and flowing along our journey.

Trying to constantly give people what they want:

> *If we can just please them,*

> **we will be safe,**
> **our needs will be met.**

> *Or so we think.*

And so we dress to impress, we paint on the smile everyone is more comfortable with, we say yes to everything, we act like we love what they love, we pretend, we perform, hoping they will accept us, and we will be safe one more day,

> *not rejected,*
> *not abandoned,*
> *not forgotten.*

Only to find after all our efforts, they are not pleased. They need more.

And so we try harder to be more, hide our emotions, and be different for them,

> constantly contorting ourselves to fit the ever-changing mold,
>> always bending, always forcing
>>> as we wonder, *when is it good enough?*

*Am **I** good enough?*

It never feels like we are.

We can't hold the smile forever. We break at times. And people scoff.

> "Wow, you're crazy."

> "You're too emotional."

And then they are gone.

They don't need someone imperfect, flawed, sad, or boring.

So, you blame yourself.

> *Why did I show any weakness?*
> *Why can't I be better?*
> *What's wrong with me?*

And you try harder once again, thinking you'll do it this time.

You will please them all.

And you will be safe.

You will be loved, wanted, protected, never recognizing the game you're in—

a losing game.

No matter how many times you start over, you think you'll get it right this time, not knowing there is no right, there is no winning,

there are no perfectly pleased people.

There is no perfect shape you can mold yourself into where you will always be wanted, always be loved and never left for something else.

The truth is, people aren't pleased by the actions of others.

They are pleased by their own thoughts and beliefs about themselves.

I had a client once who believed he was only as good as everyone *thought* he was, and he was only loved if everyone was *happy* with him.

So his brain kept note of every mistake, every misstep, every time he disappointed others. And then he blamed himself.

He thought if he was just a better person, they would be happy.

So he neglected his own needs, his own dreams, his own wants, trying to please everyone.

The problem was, they all wanted something different from him:

> his parents,
> his wife,
> his friends,
> his siblings,
> his neighbors,
> his teachers,
> and his coaches.

He made others' happiness, and unhappiness, his responsibility . . . and measured his worth by their emotions.

Which so many of us do.

This left him ultimately feeling worthless,

> *broken,*
> *disappointed,*
> *and resentful.*

He didn't have the life he desired and blamed others for it, believing he needed their approval to make his own decisions. He waited for everyone else to be pleased with his choices before allowing himself to pursue what he truly wanted.

In all of his pleasing, he became bitter, angry, and didn't feel like he knew who he was or what he liked. He created a life he hated, made choices he regretted, and became cruel and angry toward everyone he loved, not knowing who he was anymore.

He believed all of this was everyone else's fault. They "made" him do these things, "made" him angry, and "made" him live a life he didn't want.

The truth was, no one could "make" him do any of those things. They couldn't make his choices or impose feelings he didn't want to have. By trying to please everyone, he handed over his power, allowing them to have authority over his decisions and emotions. He didn't realize that all along he always had control over what he chose and who he wanted to be.

This is a clear example of how trying to please everyone can **backfire**. When you feel responsible for everyone else's emotions, you end up losing focus on your own life and goals, often leaving you feeling resentful and angry toward others.

This doesn't mean we don't care how people feel or want to help them solve their problems. This doesn't mean we are selfish. I believe we should communicate with those we love, listen to how they feel, and make decisions together with respect.

But when you lose yourself, your wants, your desires, constantly prioritizing others' expectations, your life will suffer. Every time.

Because you were created to create. It fills us with light, energy, hope, and fulfillment, which then impacts everyone else for the better.

When you create a life you love with consideration of others, you have balance and peace.

You develop trust with yourself, knowing that you will take care of your wants and needs too. This also creates love within yourself, which allows you to love others more because you aren't dependent on them, you aren't angry at them for making your choices, and you don't have to avoid them to protect yourself.

In our search for approval, we often neglect who we truly are, shapeshifting to align with external expectations. But the truth is, your worth is not measured by the satisfaction of others. Remember, you were created to bring forth your unique gifts into the world. When you show up in abundance for the life you want while considering the needs of those you love, you create not only a life of balance and peace for yourself but also an authentic connection that enriches the lives of everyone around you. You'll discover that true acceptance and love are found within, **and that's where your real power lies.**

Chapter 7

WHAT IS "LOVE"?

When you first enter this world, you are filled with trust. As a tiny newborn, you instinctively nestled into the arms of anyone who held you, completely vulnerable, trusting that you were safe without knowing anything about them. You had no fear of being dropped, having never known that kind of danger. But as you grew, life's bumps and bruises introduced you to pain and discomfort. You began to realize that people and situations are not always safe. Those initial tests of trust came in small doses and gradually expanded into bigger challenges, shaping your understanding of the world.

And over the years, you noticed people would come and go like seasons, bringing warmth or fun for a while, and then fading like the sunset, leaving you for something better. Love seemed to come and go all along the way, and as good as it felt to be loved, it felt worse to feel rejected, abandoned, or ridiculed.

Is love just a transaction? For people to come and get something from you, and once they've had enough they run to something else?

Is it just a give and take?

I thought so.

What was once a question in my mind became a belief. This is what our brains do. They look for evidence to support our thoughts and then those thoughts seem like facts over time.

My brain did this with love.

All my life I loved big. It was so easy for me. I didn't need people to be anything for me; I just loved them.

I thought everyone loved easily, readily, and always.

Until I was hurt,

> left,
> judged,
> forgotten,
> traded,
> and used.

Love started to feel so heavy for me. It seemed like everyone had some kind of condition upon which they loved me. I tried to meet all those conditions for everyone for a long time, not realizing that I was losing trust in love along the way.

Over time I was afraid to believe someone when they said, "I love you." I didn't trust it and didn't believe it could last. I thought they loved *what I did for them, not who I was*. Maybe that was true. I'll never know.

So I became good at being what people wanted so I could *earn their love*. I did this with friends, teachers, parents, boyfriends, and especially God. I would quickly figure out what they wanted or expected from me, and then I would be that for them.

I went to church and was told that God loved me unconditionally, then spent hours listening to the conditions I needed to meet to earn His love. Since everyone else's love felt conditional, I assumed God's must be too.

I paid more attention to living up to the conditions of love than actually feeling love. It felt more important to earn it than

> to feel it,
> believe it,
> or receive it.

I rarely believed anyone loved me just for me being me.

I thought if I kept all the conditions and earned love, then I would be more safe.

To the brain love feels safe, and that is why we are all desperate for it.

I didn't realize at the time that this very thing is what led to me becoming a people pleaser. I thought love was a set of equations that looked like this:

> The more I pleased people = the more they would love me.

> The less I please people = the less they would love me.

> The less they loved me = the less safe I would be.

Seems simple, right?

We don't become people pleasers because it sounds fun and interesting. We become people pleasers because we have attached people-pleasing to love and safety, which are both basic human needs.

Attaching love to people being pleased and happy with us leads us through a life of becoming anything and everything except who we want to be for ourselves.

Through many years of friendships and relationships I had to learn the hard way that people don't love you "no matter what," they don't always stay, and love isn't constant and unconditional for most people. I learned that people love and still leave or eventually change their minds, or that love required too much of me.

Over time my innocent love for everyone, and my belief that everyone loved me too, became tainted, strained, and full of doubt. After loving and losing so many times, I became resentful of love and even resistant to it. When people would tell me they loved me I would smile and nod, but I wouldn't feel anything. I didn't know how to trust it, and I didn't believe love would stay anyway.

It felt more dangerous to allow love in than to just keep myself from it altogether.

Over time it became really difficult to feel loved, and I thought it was because no one really loved me.

I didn't realize until years later that it wasn't the lack of love they felt for me, *it was my lack of trust in or acceptance of it.*

I was the only one in my own way.

I was the one not *feeling* the love, out of protection. But the truth was, I wasn't any more safe by thinking that nobody loved me.

I thought I had cracked the code and was outsmarting the pain by avoiding feeling love, until I realized I wasn't preventing pain, *I was causing it.* I wasn't feeling love—one of the best feelings in the world—not because it wasn't there but because I wouldn't *allow* myself to feel it.

Over the years, I've worked with many clients who unknowingly did the same with love. They weren't aware of it; they simply noticed a constant feeling of never being enough for anyone. They felt unloved and lived in pain. As we worked together, they came to understand that their struggle to believe others loved them stemmed from their own inability to love *themselves* as they are.

The brain's way of protecting us from pain is to avoid feeling good emotions so we don't have to face losing them later.

The brain doesn't realize that

> this just creates pain **ahead of time**. It doesn't prevent it!

Isn't that so shocking to realize!? It was for me!

I wanted to feel loved. And I thought someone just had to really mean it or prove it.

So I was looking for the lack of love in relationships. I was looking for and waiting for them to change their minds.

I didn't trust others easily, so I wasn't being myself.

I probably made it harder to love me by doing all of this.

We create what we think about over and over.

We create a lot of our pain and use it as evidence we aren't loved.

> To feel loved, *you have to believe it's there.*

To feel loved, *you have to generate it within yourself.*

To feel loved, *you have to believe you are lovable,* **worth** *loving, and enough for someone's love.*

You have to open the door and be open to receive it.

Love is always waiting on the other side—in someone, in nature, in creation, in opportunities, in you, in God. It is always there.

But if you close the door and lock it, hoping love will bust it down, chase you down the hall, and force it on you . . .

> it won't.
> It can't.
> It's a law.

We have to *allow* it in

and not fear it.

The truth is, **love never hurts**. Only the lack of love does.

No one can hand love to you. And you can't lose it accidentally.

Love lives inside the person doing the loving.

So if someone loves you, *they feel love.*

You may not feel loved when someone is loving you because you can't feel someone else's love. Only *they* can feel it.

All the movies and music have told us we can feel other people's love for us. They have convinced us we have to get it from someone, or make them love us.

But even if they do, we hold the key.

Even if they say the words, we have to believe it or not.

Even if they try to convince us with actions, service, time, or gifts, we have to see it as love, or we won't *feel* it.

We never really know how someone feels about us. We can't know. *It's theirs to feel.*

And your love for others is *yours* to feel.

- When you think loving thoughts about anyone . . . you will feel love.
- When you think loving thoughts about yourself . . . you will feel love.
- When you are grateful for others and yourself . . . you will feel love.

It's always yours to have because love is an emotion that is generated by you and your thoughts.

Allow yourself to feel it.

Let this awareness free you from the desperate chase.

Love is all around you. Look for it, believe it, and breathe it in.

Chapter 8

AGENCY

In many religions and the religion I belong to, we believe God has given us agency and that it is our greatest gift. We believe God can do anything, has all power to give and take away, but God never takes our agency (or choice).

In the religion I belong to, we believe there was a war in Heaven between God and Satan over our agency. Satan wanted to take away our choice, ensuring we would all return to Heaven in a perfect way without free will. God, on the other hand, desired for us to have the ability to choose for ourselves—the freedom and power to design our lives, make our own decisions, and experience the consequences of those choices. We believe we chose God's plan of agency with a divine purpose, and we were thrilled to come to earth to create and experience our choices, to experience, feel, and know who we wanted to be, what we wanted to do, and why.

This concept can be challenging for our human minds and egos, which often seek control and operate from a place of scarcity and fear. I learned that we chose God's plan of agency with a divine purpose, yet I've often noticed people judging others for their choices and wanting to control or force them to choose a certain way. Some even exclude or distance themselves from those whose decisions don't align with their own. Herein lies the contradiction: despite our initial excitement for the freedom of choice, we became fixated on limiting it once we were on Earth. It makes me wonder, *didn't we all embrace agency and the freedom to choose? Yet here we are, enacting Satan's plan by trying to impose our will on others*. We attempt to make others "choose the right," judge them for "wrong" decisions, and separate ourselves from those who don't follow our path. It's fascinating how we claim to cherish agency yet quickly panic when people make their own choices.

We are also taught to use our agency to make the "right" choices and to align our lives with what we believe God would want, basing our actions on our understanding of His desires.

Growing up this was difficult for my young brain to grasp. I was taught about the gift of God-given agency and the power to choose, yet I frequently heard discussions about what choices we should or shouldn't make. There were endless opinions on what constituted good or bad choices and everything in between. Instead of feeling fun and exciting, making choices became daunting, leaving me uncertain whether my decisions were always "right." I would often worry about what would happen if I made the wrong choice or not the *most right* one, imagining that God was up there shaking His head in disappointment over and over. "Don't mess it up. Don't choose wrong or *else you will be punished*." I worried that If I don't do this life experience the right way, I wouldn't live the life God intended for me, and I would experience pain and regret and miss out on the chance of living with God again.

With this thinking, agency can go from being a wonderful gift to a heavy burden really quickly for our human minds. Every choice can become so confusing because the brain is playing out hundreds of different scenarios for each choice and how each one could potentially lead to danger. The mind then spins in indecision, afraid to choose for fear it will be wrong.

We take our precious agency and give it away because it feels too heavy. We start asking other people what they would choose if they were us. We gather all kinds of opinions and ask God in prayer what we should do. We think that if someone else tells us what to do we have a better chance of getting it right and staying safe from consequences.

I have a friend who has never liked the idea of agency. She would often say, "I just wish someone else could make my decisions for me, so I don't have to be responsible for it all. It feels too scary and I don't trust myself to make the right choice all the time. I always feel like I'm doing it wrong anyway." I'll never forget when she said that. And I could see how she felt that way. The responsibility of our choices can often be too heavy of a burden to bear, so **we live in fear rather than freedom**. Instead of feeling empowered to make our own decisions, agency begins to feel dangerous, and keeps us small.

Agency can feel like being given a beautifully wrapped gift that is promised to contain everything you want and desire. It's offered to you out of love, meant to be yours forever, with the assurance that it will never be taken back. Filled with excitement and anticipation, you hold this gift that is wrapped in gold paper. You can't wait to open it, experience the magic, and let it transform your life in countless ways! And just as you are about to open it, the giver of the gift says, "Oh, just so you know, this is a very important gift, but don't use it the wrong way, don't mess it up, and make sure you always do what is right with it, 'k?" You stare at the gift, your excitement is still there, but you are a little more nervous and even hesitant to open it. You reply, "OK, I'll use it correctly, and I won't mess it up, but how will I know if I mess it up, and what will happen if I do?" The gift giver doesn't have any specific rules, whys, or hows, and says, "Just choose the right, and you will be happy."

This gift starts to feel heavier in your hand. You start to feel more anxious than excited. You have more questions than answers. You aren't sure you want to be responsible for such a gift as this. You don't totally understand how this works; there seem to be no rules yet very important ones at the same time, and no one can tell you exactly what they are.

You open the gift of agency and start to overthink every choice, wondering if it's the right one, and not just the right one but the rightest right one and the bestest best one. You begin overthinking big decisions and small, over time feeling scared to choose for fear it's wrong, seeking for permission and approval from others so you can triple check that you're using this gift correctly. But they all have different thoughts, ideas, and opinions about what is right and what they would choose.

Everyone seems to be making all kinds of different choices with their own gift, choices that you thought were wrong, choices you wouldn't make, yet they seem content with their choices. It gets more and more confusing. You often wonder, *how did we all receive the same gift, with the same rules but use it so differently?* Some people choose to dream and create new ideas in the world with their gift while others choose to earn a degree and work for someone else. Some choose to eat whatever tastes the best for every meal while others meticulously count calories and measure grams to ensure they eat "just right." Some choose to exercise to exhaustion and feel that is the most right way to be strong and healthy while some prefer walking, yoga, and eating intuitively. Some worship God within the walls of a church, following guidelines and structure, while others find spiritual connection through nature and meditation. You notice many people choosing to get married and have a family while others stay single and take care of themselves. Some people prioritize spending money on adventures and vacations while others view fun as a waste and prefer to save their extra cash for emergencies.

Everyone received the same gift, but no one uses it the same way.

If we looked at all the choices everyone has made for themselves, how would we ever know which person was doing it "right"? We all have different thoughts and beliefs about what choices are right and wrong. We are all playing the same game but with different rules about what decisions are right and wrong. This is why we all live very different lives filled with different choices, experiences, and outcomes.

Our brains assume that everyone should play by the same rules we have for ourselves, that everyone should use their gift of agency the same way, that our own idea of what is "right" *is right for all*. This makes it so easy to judge everyone and think they are doing it "wrong" because they live differently.

But if we believe God gave us choice and never takes it away—and He gave it knowing there are millions of choices, endless options, and more "rights" than we can comprehend—**maybe God trusts that what we choose will give us the experience we came here to have,** that our choice should be so unique and so individual that no two people choose the same things, that because of choice, no one in all the billions of people live the exact same life. Because of the gift of agency, the world is filled with differences, wonder, and a myriad of creations.

Each artist creates something unique, and no matter how many artists there are, they never create the same thing. Their unique choices, desires, and ideas lead to intricate pieces, each one distinct. It's truly fascinating.

The brain has a hard time understanding abundance. It likes to be able to fit all the possibilities and answers into boxes so agency can be contained and fully understood. But agency is too vast to be contained in a box.

God gave us this gift in trust, knowing that what we choose for ourselves would be what we *need*. God doesn't choose for us; God allows the choice with a purpose we may never understand here on Earth.

I believe that what you desire to create, what you dream about, the things that fill you with light, hope, and love are yours to choose. I believe that your "right" choice will be different from someone else's, that when we allow ourselves to choose as God does, we won't keep overthinking and second-guessing everything and staying stuck in fear of making the wrong choice.

All of my life I heard people around me say things like,

> "I don't know what to do. I don't want to make the wrong choice." or
> "I want to do what's right."

I saw people spin in indecision constantly, wondering what God wanted them to choose, *who* God wanted them to marry and *when*, constantly asking for other people's opinions on what they should or shouldn't do, only to feel paralyzed by the fear of making the wrong choice and disrupting God's plan for them or facing a painful consequence.

I watched people making decisions based on what their parents, friends, teachers, and everyone else—except for themselves—wanted, believing others knew better. Soon after, disappointment would follow. Whether marrying someone they didn't truly love because it pleased others, starting a family to relieve pressure from family, studying a subject in college just to make their parents proud, or staying in a job they despised to avoid upsetting their spouse—the list goes on and on—I watched as they handed over their precious gift of agency, allowing everyone else to choose for them.

Only to realize years later they weren't living a life *they* wanted, or having results that *they* were proud of.

This left them frustrated, angry, resentful, and depressed, constantly asking themselves, *How did I get here?*

And over time I realized that when you defer your agency to others, **you forfeit your power to create your life on purpose**. When you let others choose for you, you keep getting results and consequences *you don't want*.

This is depressing, and it should be because you are living outside of yourself. You are giving up your choice, which makes life seem unjust and never what you wanted it to be.

About five years ago, I took my husband to Jody Moore's live coaching event. I had been listening to her podcast for a year or two and loved what she taught about the brain and how to create your life through the power of thinking. I was thrilled that she was coming to the city where I lived, and I was ready to absorb all her incredible wisdom. I vividly remember the seat I sat in, the color of the carpet, and the words she wrote on the whiteboard while coaching a woman in the front row. I knew nothing about how Jody became a coach, the training she underwent, or how she acquired her knowledge. I just knew I loved it and was utterly fascinated by it. And then I had a simple thought:

I want to do that!

As that thought lingered, a wave of emotion ran from my head down to my toes. I felt alive, excited, and determined, like I knew this was for me. I knew that this was what I was meant to do. Nothing lit me up like this did.

That thought alone generated curiosity and excitement, which led me to figuring out how to become a coach. It wasn't long before I enrolled in the same life coaching school and then went through Jody Moore's advanced coach-training program where I became a coach myself.

There was a moment in my home office when I was coaching a client, using the same model on a whiteboard, just as I had seen Jody do years earlier at her live event. In that instant, the memory of sitting in that chair, thinking, *I want to do that* flooded my mind. And there I was, doing exactly what I had once dreamed of.

That one thought alone has created so many incredible results in my life. This is how I create the life I want to live, experiencing the things that light me up, fuel me forward, and give me purpose.

I simply allow myself to want, and I trust that my wants are good. My decisions are mine to make, and the only way to create the life I desire to live is by using my agency for me, not giving it to anyone else. **When I let others choose for me, as I have in the past, I lived a life that they wanted, not the life I wanted.**

It was less than a year ago that I saw Keira Brinton taking people who had never written books to far-off places to write a book in five days. Once more, I found myself captivated, observing and contemplating what it would be like and whether I could do it. I distinctly remember having the same thought,

I want to do that!

I didn't have experience, I didn't know Keira, and I had never considered writing a book.

But I had the desire to do it, and that was enough motivation for me to find a way.

And now I find myself nestled in the awe-inspiring Muir Woods in California—a place I've never been before—surrounded by towering, ancient trees, writing my first book alongside two other authors who were strangers just days ago. All of this is happening simply because I dared to try, to step into the unknown and choose something that no one would have ever chosen for me.

No one that knows me understands why I'm here writing a book. None of them would have told me I *should* do this. This isn't something they would choose to do for themselves. So I didn't ask for anyone's permission. I didn't ask if anyone thought I *should* do this; I didn't need their opinions because my life isn't theirs, nor theirs mine.

This is how I create my life. And you're allowed to do the same.

Your wants are good, your dreams are good. Your choices are yours to make; use them to create the life you want to live. Move your feet, and allow God to guide you. God wants you to live in a way that ignites your spirit so you can experience creation as God does.

You aren't messing it up.

You are creating a unique experience for yourself, and you are allowed that.

You are free.

Chapter 9

THE TUG-OF-WAR

Have you ever played tug-of-war? I remember loving this game when I was growing up. We would divide up into two even teams, and each team would pick up one side of a long rope. The center of the rope was marked with red tape, and there were two lines a few feet out from the center. Each team was supposed to pull the center of the rope across the line to their side, and whichever team did it won.

It's a simple game with straightforward rules. As soon as you pick up your end of the rope and hear the word "go!" you pull as if your life depends on it. Each time, players dig in their heels and pull with all their might, hands blistering, faces sweating, unwilling to let go or give up.

Our brains and our egos love to play tug-of-war in relationships as well. And it does end up feeling like a war when we do this.

We engage in this behavior when we try to influence someone to make decisions that align with our own desires. We pick up the rope and pull, trying to convince them of what they should or shouldn't do, giving all kinds of reasons and evidence of why we are right.

When you try to control or take away another person's agency, much like in the game of tug-of-war you will encounter resistance!

We don't even recognize the intense battle we are creating by trying to control and manipulate others' choices.

Think about a time when someone tried to compel you to do something—even if it was something you normally wouldn't mind doing. The moment they try to force, convince, or use guilt to get you to do it, you immediately lose all desire to do that thing. You resist because of the opposing force of the pull. You are no longer resisting the action they requested, you are resisting your loss of agency.

The gift to choose is given to us from the Divine, and when any person tries to take our choice, force us, pull us, or make our choices for us—we resist, instinctively protecting our agency and our choices for our lives.

Take a moment to think of something you really enjoy, like ice cream. When you get to choose when to indulge, it's delicious and satisfying. You might even crave it so much that you'd drive across town for a scoop. But imagine if someone forced you into your favorite ice cream shop, handcuffed you to an ice cream machine, and made you eat only ice cream for a week. Would you still crave ice cream? Would it still feel exciting and satisfying?

No!

You would quickly despise ice cream, and once free from the ice cream shop, you'd likely never want to return because when we are forced to do something—it doesn't matter what it is, it doesn't matter if we like it—we will resist it.

On the flip side, if you really enjoy eating ice cream and I continually insist that you **shouldn't** eat it ever again—explaining all the reasons it's bad for you and judging you every time you indulge, trying to convince you to do it my way—your urge and desire for ice cream would just intensify! You would find yourself thinking about where the nearest ice cream shop is and how quickly you could satisfy that craving.

Just like in tug-of-war, it doesn't matter what someone is trying to pull you toward. If they force you to eat ice cream, you'll avoid it. But if they keep trying to stop you from having it, you'll crave it even more and go to great lengths to get it. When someone grabs the rope and tries to pull you over to their side—to make choices for you—you'll automatically resist.

The same goes for religion. If you love your religion and want people to feel the way you do about it, your brain may pick up the rope and try to prove, convince, and force them to join your church.

You might try to tell them how much you love it and then invite them. If they don't come, you may try to tell them how they missed out and they *should* have come. If that doesn't work, you may try using incentives to bribe them into coming. And over time you may try to even use fear to get them to come, telling them what will happen to their soul, and that they won't go to heaven if they don't join you at church.

You can pull and pull.

But they will resist.

A much better way to invite someone to anything is to offer, and let them choose.

If you are experiencing resistance in any of your relationships, you might be playing tug-of-war and not realizing it.

Save your energy and sanity and stop trying to pull everyone to where you want them to go, knowing you don't like that either.

Put the rope down, take a breath, and realize that all of us like to choose for ourselves.

God knew that choice was imperative to our human experience.

One of the greatest gifts we can give those we love is to set our end of the rope down and stop pulling them to decisions we believe they should make. By releasing the rope and allowing others the freedom to choose and then experience consequence, resistance and arguing fade away. Instead, we make space for connection and mutual respect. **This allows us to ask more questions, really listen, and strive to understand before making assumptions. With greater context, we can share our suggestions, and the other person can truly consider our opinions and ideas without feeling the need to protect their agency. Together, you can work toward finding solutions much faster.** Trust in the God-given power of choice—not just for yourself but for those you care about. Let go of the urge to control and discover the peace that comes with honoring each person's unique choices.

Remember, the divine gift of choice is the foundation of unconditional love.

Section 2

MOTHERS:
THE CREATORS OF LIFE

WITHOUT WOMEN, THERE IS NO CREATION, FOR THERE WOULD BE NO PEOPLE TO CREATE.

Chapter 10

WHO IS GOD?

I grew up believing I had to *earn* God's love by doing everything people said He wanted, so I could be blessed, protected, and loved by Him.

My young mind imagined that God must be similar to Santa Claus:

> *making a list, and checking it twice, trying to find out who's naughty or nice.*

I imagined God up there, delighted in tallying my good and bad deeds, adding them up each day to see if I was in the green or the red, determining if I was good or bad, and deciding if I deserved a punishment or a reward.

A trial or a blessing.

All my life I have learned about and prayed to Heavenly Father, a Father who created me and sent me here to learn. It felt peaceful and filled me with hope that there was a perfect being watching over and protecting me.

I prayed every single night at the side of my bed. And as I prayed, I would imagine a Father only, a man who loved me but was also testing me. I believed I needed to please this man who needed me to "get it right."

Like most brains, my brain imagined Him in some ways to be like my own father. Because we can't see God the Father, our brains have to guess, assume, and fill in the blanks with things we know about fathers. This is how *we create* God in our minds. We all think we believe in the same version of God.

But we don't.

We can't.

Our brains draw from our personal experiences and knowledge to envision God. In our minds, each of us forms a unique image of God, shaped by what we hope He is, what we need Him to be, the traits we admire in our own fathers, and notions we've heard from others. I combined the qualities I loved about my own father with the fears and scarcity I've heard from others.

So *my* God was a Father only, because that's what I was taught, that's all I heard. He sent me here, He loved me, He wanted me to return to Him. So I imagined a kind but stern Father, one who wasn't happy often because we were all down here messing it up and being anything but perfect, doing things we shouldn't. I pictured a Father who had strict rules, who knew everything but lived in scarcity. His love, grace, forgiveness, help, and joy were not enough for everyone, only those that kept the commandments and were close to perfect.

Because I believed that I had to earn His love with my actions, I never felt like I was good enough. Because God is perfect, how could I ever live up to perfection? How could I please someone I couldn't see, couldn't fully understand or imagine? I wanted to feel loved by God like so many others talked about, but I couldn't feel loved when I was so focused on doing everything "right."

Many of my parents' beliefs, personality traits, strengths, and weaknesses got intermingled with my view of God. I think most of our brains do that. They take what they understand about their parents and *copy and paste* it onto God.

There are millions of different versions of God in the imaginations of our minds.

There were a handful of times at church when I heard of Heavenly *Parents*, and that there was a Father *and* a Mother in Heaven, but it seemed to be skimmed over quickly without much information about the Mother. Most of the religious language I heard talked about God *as a Father only, and I never really heard of a religion in all the world that believed there was a Mother God.*

So, of course, when I prayed or thought of how I came to exist on this planet, I imagined a man creating me with his hands—not with his body, or through pain and suffering. I thought it was probably easy, maybe even fun and magical. When I was young, I pictured God creating humans on a conveyor belt just to see how many He could make!

I couldn't imagine how a man made children other than in some inhuman, magical way because on earth, women create life through pregnancy and birth. It's obvious. We all see it, we all know it, and we don't question it.

But if you mention that maybe a woman took part in our creation in Heaven, our brains explode. We get all uncomfortable and quiet, *like we are breaking some holy rule by speaking such blasphemy.*

Any time I would ask about having a Divine Mother in Heaven, people's voices would get soft, like a whisper, and they'd say, "Yeah, the Church says we have a mother there, but we just shouldn't talk about Her." And it would get awkward really quickly. If I asked why we didn't talk about Her, no one knew why. They would say, "I don't know. I think it's because She is too sacred to talk about. The Father is protecting Her so we don't use Her name in vain."

You could see how confusing this was to a young girl's mind, and I couldn't quite make sense of all of this—the quiet whispers, the discomfort, the pale faces, like we were going to be in trouble for speaking of a Mother.

A Mother!

Like it was taboo and we were breaking the rules.

I often just took their word for it and thought maybe She *is* protected from us. Maybe we are *that* bad, that even mentioning Her would be disrespectful.

So I tried to not think of Her. I tried to not ask or speak about Her. I wanted to obey the rules and avoid causing her pain with my thoughts of Her. I tried to protect Her from my imperfect human self. And I often thought, *well, maybe Heavenly Father can better handle all of us flawed, unruly, bad children. Thank goodness He will deal with us so She doesn't have to.*

How nice of Him.

But in the back of my mind I would wonder, *why is a Divine Mother so taboo?* And *why am I so bad that She wouldn't want me to think of or speak to Her? Am I such a disappointment that speaking to me would ruin Her glory and taint her divinity?*

I had never encountered anyone in the world who was so loved and respected that their name was never mentioned, and they were never spoken of because of a fear that they might become known.

It was like that rule only applied to Her. She was too special to be known, too sacred to be praised.

I tried to let that answer satisfy me. I tried and tried because, of course, I didn't want to be the one that spoke of Her and freaked everyone out. Remember how much I tried to make sure people were perfectly pleased? Mentioning Her seemed to do the very opposite of pleasing people. Even writing about Her now makes me nervous, which is so strange, *but I feel uncomfortable!*

I keep asking myself if I should erase this part and just talk about something everyone is comfortable with and can agree on.

I didn't want to speak of Her if God would be mad at me for it like I had always thought He would.

I didn't want to cause anyone harm. I just wanted to know where She was, if She knew me, if She loved me, if She cared about or understood anything I had experienced as a woman.

I tried to keep Her out of my mind, out of my mouth, and out of my prayers—just like everyone else did— to protect Her from me.

Because a "natural man is an enemy to God,"[1] as they say.

I must be Her enemy then. *Maybe that's it?* God the Father has to protect our Mother from us because we are the enemy. And if we talk to Her, we will defile Her. Our mere words would taint Her.

---

[1] "Mosiah 3:19," *The Book of Mormon*, The Church of Jesus Christ of Latter-day Saints.

How could this be?

I never could understand it. It was like my soul knew something wasn't right.

What kind and loving mother doesn't want to be known or spoken of by Her children? How could She ever wish that they didn't know She existed? Would She really hope that they would never talk to her or about Her? Did She really need to be shielded by their Father as a barricade from Her children?

This whole idea caused a lot of confusion for me as a little girl: growing up constantly learning about Heavenly Father, how He made us, and loves us, and gave a us life; that we should be ever so grateful for His sacrifice for us; that we should praise Him and honor Him.

And I did.

But it felt like I had to *or else.*

Like our Heavenly Father needed our love, needed us to get it right, needed us to prove our devotion through our daily prayers, daily scripture study, being kind, telling the truth, working hard, praying daily, and doing right. Never make a wrong choice or play on Sunday. Never feel angry or ungrateful. And for *sure* never doubt anything because then you must not have any faith or believe in Him.

It felt like Heavenly Father needed so much. He needed our time, our attention, our sacrifice, our prayers, our study, our perfect faith, and our church attendance—everything to be checked off regularly to prove our devotion and love.

And I lived like that. Oh, how I tried to live like that.

But I almost never felt loved. The love didn't seem like it was about me or *for me at all*.

It was like I only existed to make sure Heavenly Father knew *I* loved *Him*.

He needed me to, for some reason.

And as a people pleaser, I tried to please, and please, and please.

But of course, it was never enough,

Because I wasn't enough.

How many times did I think, *I got it ALL right from the long list of to dos proving I loved God*?

Never.

Not one day.

I tried so hard to pray in the perfect order, only being grateful, asking little, saying "thy will be done," and sorry for everything else—sorry for existing and being a human, so human that You have to protect me from my Mother so I don't cause Her pain just by Her knowing me.

My prayers became apologies and saying how grateful I was for everything else—good or bad, and saying sorry for feeling any emotion that wasn't positive

 because that was what I thought was required for Him to love me.

Something was always required, and no matter how nice I was, how much I accomplished, or how I felt for other people, it was never enough.

My brain was trained to see the lack and find the imperfection in myself because if I didn't, I was prideful and conceited.

So, of course I couldn't feel like I was enough for God this way, because it's God! God is perfect, God *is* enough. God is never too much or too little of anything.

But I was.

I was too loud *and* too quiet. I was right *and* I was wrong. I was forgetful, and I was late to almost everything. I was too much for some *and* too little for others.

So how could all my doings ever add up to being enough for a perfect Father, a Father that demands so much from someone so small?

At times I allowed myself to dream of a Mother in Heaven, just so I could feel some warmth, comfort, and safety. You know when you're scared or overwhelmed and you just want to curl up in your mother's lap and be held? Not judged or criticized, just loved. As her child. A child that She carried and birthed—flesh of her flesh—someone who knows you best and has loved you even when you couldn't do anything right.

I would imagine Her up there so bright, so brilliant, made of the purest love that existed.

And I would believe She was mine and I was Hers.

And She didn't need to be protected from me, and maybe—just maybe—I wasn't dangerous to Her. I wasn't so bad that She didn't want to talk to me.

There were people in my life that I wasn't good enough for. I knew people that didn't want to listen to me because I wasn't interesting enough, or I said the wrong words in the wrong way. I knew rejection, and I knew it well.

So being told that my Mother needed to be protected from me made me feel that rejection down to my cells. Why did you create me if you don't want me as I am?

I didn't make me.

I didn't give myself this body and imperfections.

I don't want to be this way either, but *I* didn't make me.

I was trying desperately to earn Heavenly Father's love, only to experience disappointment at the end of each day because I had failed. Even if I didn't know exactly how, I knew I must have.

This made me focus on all that I *wasn't* instead of all that I **was**.

My brain, which is designed to protect me from physical and emotional danger, tried to come up with ways to protect me from losing God's love.

And because I had always thought it had to be earned by perfect doings, I went to work trying to earn it.

I was constantly told that living with Heavenly Father is the ultimate goal, the ultimate happiness and safety.

So I believed that I must be perfect to be safe. To be with God, we have to work really hard, we have to get this life exactly right, we have to be anything but an imperfect human somehow, even though we are always told we are imperfect humans.

The cognitive dissonance really does a number on us.

Examples of this from what I heard are:

> "You are loved unconditionally no matter what . . . but also get all the conditions right so you will be loved and let into Heaven, 'K?!'"

> "God is plural, meaning Father and Mother. But remember, we only talk about and pray to the Father; your Mother is there, but we don't know where She is. Also, don't mention Her because then Father will get mad."

> "You were created in the image of God, which is only a Man, even though you are a woman."

Isn't it so confusing?

No wonder so many of us never feel like we are doing it right for God. No wonder we hyperfocus on our weaknesses and mistakes, because our brains think that will help us be more perfect and then ultimately make it to Heaven where we will be loved and safe.

The brain is highly committed to love and safety, which are more important to us than anything else because the brain sees safety as our **survival**.

If we are taught the conditions to get to that safety, we will achieve them the best we can.

There were times I would pause and wonder, *do I really want to live in this Heaven with this God? This Father that I am desperately trying to please and never feel I am good enough for? This man that somehow created me by Himself and doesn't want me to know I have a Mother? A Father that needs all the praise and doesn't want to share any of it with Her?*

That didn't sound like love, peace, freedom, or safety! Especially for me as a woman.

So why was I working so hard to go somewhere that didn't feel loving or safe?

Either I had to try not to go to Heaven to spare myself the discomfort of living with a Father that felt so narcissistic, or I had to change how I *thought* about God.

And I had to allow myself to speak to my Mother too.

Who could stop me, really? If no one knew, no one would freak out. No one got all pale and awkward, as long as they didn't know.

I could allow Her to live in my mind, in my heart, and in my soul.

My soul knew—it always knew—that She was there.

And as long as nobody knew this about me, all was well. It looked how it should on the surface. I prayed how I was supposed to, I spoke how I was supposed to about God. I played by the rules as far as anyone could see.

But inside myself I knew that our Mother didn't need to be protected from ANY of Her children.

And as a mother myself, I love when my children come to me, speak to me, allow me in, and know I am a safe place for them. This gives me the greatest joy! It doesn't inconvenience or pain me. It is what I want most as a mother who has given my life to create theirs.

I wondered, *if I feel this way about my children as the creator and giver of their lives, maybe She does too.*

This was a love I never understood before I was a mother, so I didn't believe I could be loved this way. I couldn't believe it existed because I had not experienced it myself.

So, of course I thought love had to be earned. Of course it felt scarce and depended on my earnings and provings. Of course I thought I had to work for it, and of course it always felt fleeting because at the end of every day, focusing on all that was imperfect, I was aware of what more I could have done.

But the moment I became a mother, I understood a new kind of love, a love coming *from* me, not a love I was trying to earn.

A love for a child that did nothing to earn this love I felt. A love for a child I didn't yet know and who had only caused me pain.

But the love felt so full, so complete, so perfect without earning or doing.

I'll never forget this one moment: I stood tired at my sink, brushing my teeth for the day, when a clear thought struck me.

I heard:

> "You cannot love *more than* God. God *is* love, and if you love your children like this, imagine how God your Divine Mother loves you."

I felt a warmth pour through my veins from the top of my head down through my toes, like the hot sun warming my body from top to bottom. It made sense, like all the puzzle pieces were coming together: all the times I thought I had to earn God's love by making perfectly right decisions, all the times I wondered if I was enough, all the times I was afraid to talk to God because I thought He was disappointed.

All of the fear, scarcity, not enoughness, worry, doubt, melted away as I thought of a Mother, a Mother who is like me in some ways, who loved me in the way I loved my children—but possibly even more, even bigger, even more completely.

A love like that finally felt safe!

A love that I knew, experienced, and understood as a mother. But *for* me! Not just from me to my children, but from Her to Me!

Imagining a Divine Mother who felt intense, constant, and perfect love for me, changed me. In that simple moment while brushing my teeth, I learned the most profound lesson. I learned that the love I craved all of my life—the love that you dream about and hope for, the love that comes easily and lasts forever, the love that exists as you exist, a love you can rest in and feel safe—is a Mother's love.

I started considering, imagining, and then believing it was safe to think of Her, allowing myself to imagine Her as I prayed, thinking She loved me as I loved my children—in all my mess, imperfection, and neediness; in all my inefficiency and inconvenience; when I color outside the lines and spill the milk; when I complain and don't want to do what needs to be done; when I am not grateful for all She has done for me, and I cry when things don't feel fair; when I am forgetful and late; when I burn the casserole, and my house is a mess; when I am not productive, and I'm filled with doubt.

She gets it—maybe She has been there too—and She loves me still, as *I* love *my* children in all of their mess.

I love them *because* I created them. I love them *because* they exist. They came from me, and I sacrificed all that was important to the world to bring them here—time, money, health, energy, body image, freedom, and independence—because of love. They were mine and I was theirs. And it didn't matter what they did every day. It didn't even matter if they loved me back. It didn't matter what they said or how they said it. I loved them so completely without needing anything in return.

When I realized I was loved this way, too, everything changed.

When I thought about the Divine Mother and made space for Her in my soul and my mind, my whole energy changed.

> *My cells changed.*
> *My heart changed.*
> *My love for myself and others changed.*
> *My judgment changed.*
> *My walls started to fall.*
> *My fear started to melt away.*
> *My anxiety dissipated.*
> *My mind expanded.*
> *And peace entered.*
> *I became more loving, happy, and hopeful.*

I saw myself differently. I was no longer just a woman, lost and confused, trying to earn a Father's love.

I was a woman on her way to becoming a Goddess, like She is.

I was a woman who didn't have to people please and stay small, a woman who didn't need anyone's permission or acceptance, a woman at peace with herself, a woman who knew she was enough—even more than enough, actually—a woman who created all the time

before having children and after.

A woman who not only brought life to the earth through such pain and sacrifice, **but with such incredible strength.**

A woman who didn't need to apologize for existing, or to be more like the boys to be enough.

A woman who looked in the mirror and smiled instead of picking herself apart and only seeing flaws.

Because I saw Her in me, and me in Her.

I saw that She was never hidden, really. She lived and breathed in me, with me, every minute of every day.

When I allowed myself (without anyone's permission) to even "think" about a Mother as a God, it changed everything for me.

Everything.

And that is why I am here, typing these words, page after page

so it can change you too.

If knowing Her transformed everything for me emotionally, spiritually, physically, and mentally, I can't keep it to myself. I have to tell you too.

For so long I have felt called to tell you, but I was too afraid—afraid of what people would think, afraid to speak Her name, afraid to break the rules, afraid of all the awkward conversations and having to explain myself.

Afraid of rejection and loss of respect.

But when I think of Her, it all melts away

because She is Love.

She doesn't need to be protected by Heavenly Father. He loves Her, listens to Her, admires Her, and I believe He feels joy when She is known.

She is power, glory, divinity, and everlasting.

She doesn't need to be hidden, for She is not fragile.

She can handle all of Her children and not break.

And so can I.

As a mother, I know. I live this too.

The truth always was, and is

> She lives and breathes with her children;
> She is not hidden;
> She is not far away;
> She is not disappointed in us;
> She doesn't need us to be anything other than *who we are*.

I was never not enough for Her, just like my children will never not be enough for me.

This is how we finally let go of worrying, wondering, and fearing we are not good enough.

It is the love of a mother that heals all wounds.

It is the love of a mother that wants the deepest, richest part of ourselves

> perfectly worthy, perfectly valuable, just as we are.

The love of our Divine Mother.

Chapter 11

THE LOVE OF A MOTHER

You weren't created wrong. You aren't broken or incomplete. As a woman, you have the power of creation. All humans do. But you, *you* have the divine power of *creating life within you*. You are a portal from Heaven to Earth.

All the humans that ever have been or ever will be are birthed through women.

Think of the role of a mother. Think of what she goes through and experiences to create life. See the contrast of what a woman experiences versus what a man experiences in the process of creating a new life.

Do they experience the same thing in that process?

Or does one carry a more intense role?

One is not better than the other. That's not what I'm talking about.

Women give up their bodies, their health, their sleep, their sanity, their independence, their comfort to bring life to the earth.

But when we think, imagine, and speak of God as a singular male who created Heaven, Earth, and all of us—single-handedly, without a woman, without *Her*— does that make any sense to what we know and see here?

Have you ever seen a man create a child alone?

Have you ever seen him create *everything by himself?*

- order
- beauty
- gentleness
- design
- caregiving
- life

If we take women out of the equation, we don't have an earth, nor people to live on it, and therefore no man or woman to create *anything*. There would be

- no life,
- no death,
- no dancing,
- no dreaming,
- no buildings, paintings, or businesses.

Without women, there is no creation.

For we create ALL creators.

When we fail to recognize a woman as a divine being, we disregard the very one we know as a creator.

How do we not see it?

Do we actually think we were molded from clay?

A man just sitting comfortably in a chair grabbed some clay and carved us?

- no morning sickness
- no throwing up on the hour for nine months
- no weight gain or weight loss
- no backaches or heartburn
- no sleepless nights
- no anxiety or depression
- no loss of joy
- no suffering
- no sacrifice
- no birth
- NO change in His physical appearance, hormones, or mental state

Just clay . . .

Easy, peaceful, enjoyable?

On Earth we see the truth and know the truth. We all witness the power of creation that comes through women. But for some reason we are OK with that being deleted from our experience with God.

I am not negating God as a man.

I am only suggesting that there is *also* a Divine Mother, One who sees us, loves, and created us too.

Maybe we wouldn't doubt ourselves so much if we knew there was a Divine Feminine Being who knows what it's like to exist as a woman.

Maybe men cannot grasp a mother's kind of love, for they never experienced the pain, sacrifice, aching, and loneliness of creating life. They don't have to survive pregnancy with a huge belly, nausea, back pain, sweating, and just praying to make it through another day.

All for one child, one life.

If they don't know the pain, how can they feel the depth of the love? I don't know, and I'm not here to say they don't love just as deeply.

But I am saying the experience is not the same.

Women are given this role in creation because of their strength, because of their expansiveness and unconditional love.

For the love of a Divine Mother knows no condition. This love doesn't have to be earned.

Nor can it be.

It is perfect, unwavering, and fierce.

This kind of love will have a mother diving in front of a bus to save her child.

This love will have a mother sleeping on the floor next to a child that had a bad dream.

This love is willing to wipe bums, clean up vomit, wash dishes, do mountains of laundry, and cook a million meals a day only to have to clean up again, all so her children will have what they need.

This love spends countless hours a day in complete service.

The pain doesn't end when a child is born.

This love knows pain, oh how it knows pain,

> *the pain a mother feels when her child falls, cries, or gets hurt. It's that gut-wrenching feeling when her child gets lost for just three seconds at the grocery store, or the heartbreak when her child doesn't make the team, fails a test, loses a friend, and faces all the struggles of life. This pain runs deep, as if it's happening to her own heart.*

Her children's pain is her pain; they are flesh of her flesh.

She carries it day after day while she is trying to halfway take care of herself, and only after they have been taken care of.

It is the most Godlike love I know.

And before I became a mother, I knew it had to exist. I dreamed of someone loving me this way.

And the second I heard my first child take his first breath, I felt that love that I once dreamed of fill my whole body, like lava from my head to my toes—complete and whole, nothing lacking.

> *Before I ever saw my child's face,*
> *when I heard his first breath, and then a cry,*
> *I knew I would do anything to keep giving him life.*

It's a love that can't even be written about with words, for it is not of this earth. It makes no sense to the mind because this love doesn't need any doing or any proving.

My children have never, nor could ever, *earn* this love from me.

They take and take. It is completely consuming and exhausting to just keep them alive. They make nothing easier or lighter for me.

They are fully human, imperfect all day long.

They get almost nothing right.

And I don't need them to. I don't want them to.

And this love—

> it doesn't fade,

> it doesn't lessen.

No matter what they do or don't do,

> *it stays.*

Even as I scrape gum off my new couch and scrub pee out of my rug, even as I meticulously fold all their clothes, only for them to toss them onto the ground and jump joyfully in the pile,

> **this love stays.**

They undo everything I do.

And I get up and do it again, because of *this* love,

> *the love of a mother.*

We cannot erase Her, for we would erase the knowing of this love.

For this love eradicates self-doubt and not enoughness.

Those thoughts and feelings never came from Her. You are Her child, Her creation. The time She spent creating you . . . can you even imagine? Can you even comprehend the knowingness She has for you on a cellular level and down to your very soul?

Removing our Divine Mother from our language is what brings in doubt, fear, insecurity, and never feeling enough for anything or anyone.

Removing our Mother from our thoughts creates this deep desperation in women to need approval and acceptance from a man.

It makes love seem scarce and makes us believe that we are never enough for it.

This makes women become needy for attention and cheap affection,

- getting into unhealthy relationships and staying in them because they don't know who they are without him;
- craving approval—from their friends, husband, and their own children—in every social gathering and family setting, because they've never known who they are, who they always were, and who they will be.

And it gives us all the underlying belief that if God is man then man is God, which leads to narcissistic abuse, gaslighting, and controlling and demeaning behavior from men. When men believe they are God, but women are not, it leads to unhealthy, unloving behaviors.

It can result in men not respecting women or valuing their ideas. Such men make significant family decisions without considering a woman's input, viewing her as belonging to them, existing to meet their needs. They expect her to fulfill their conditions and serve them, without reciprocating.

If men recognized and truly believed in a Divine Mother—imagining and worshiping God as their Mother too—they might respect and value women's voices and ideas as essential, not optional. Imagine a world where family decisions are made together, with equal voices at the table, and where women are seen as complete individuals, not as extensions of someone else. Embracing the Divine Feminine could transform relationships into partnerships grounded in mutual respect and love. If we understood that God is both a Father and a Mother, what do you think would change in society?

I believe almost everything.

Chapter 12

BECOMING A MOTHER

I first realized I had only ever been taught about having a Father in Heaven when I had my third baby. My first two children were boys, and their arrivals had been planned and prepared for.

But my last baby wasn't planned. I wasn't ready to have another child. I wasn't even thinking about it. I had wanted more children, but I didn't want to ever go through pregnancy again. My pregnancies were the hardest thing I had ever been through.

It was only five weeks into my pregnancy when the familiar nausea hit. I started throwing up in the morning and would continue throughout the day. Everyone told me it was normal, not to worry, it's fine, this is "just" morning sickness.

And by the way, congratulations, you're pregnant!

I told myself it was good news, and that I guess somehow that meant it was a healthy pregnancy. *Or so they said.*

I threw up twelve or more times every day and night. If I rolled over in bed, I would throw up. If I got up to pee, I would throw up. If I even heard the sound of my husband spraying cologne in the bathroom in the morning, I would throw up.

Food was a chore instead of a pleasure. It all tasted like rusty metal. I would choke down what I could and then throw it up before I finished my last bite.

I would go to my OB appointments and ask the doctor about this sickness. "Should I be throwing up this much? I can't eat or sleep. I carry a metal bowl with me in the car and plastic bags in my purse because I throw up everywhere I go. I feel too sick and depressed. I can't do anything."

She'd smile and, with a little giggle, assure me everything was fine and dandy, pat me on the back and congratulate me on a healthy pregnancy.

I was *so* confused!

How is everyone around me OK with this?

How come no one is concerned?

Everywhere I would go, people would congratulate me as if I'd won something amazing.

It felt like I was slowly dying—losing sleep, losing my mind, losing myself.

Nothing sounded fun anymore. Nothing *was* fun anymore. I didn't want to go shopping or out to lunch for fear I would throw up in public. I had no energy. Everything was hard. So hard.

But no one's lives around me stopped. Everyone else was fine.

My husband still woke up in the morning,

>went to the gym then to work,
>ate what sounded good on the menu,
>and slept just fine through the night.

And I love my husband. He was helpful and so kind. He would often hold my hair in the night while I threw up profusely. He would make me anything that sounded edible. He would push on pressure points on the bottom of my feet until his fingers were numb because it relieved the nausea for a few minutes. And he would buy me all the anti-nausea medicine he could find at the store.

How could I blame or hate him? What more could he do?

But I couldn't help but notice how his life didn't change like mine did.

I couldn't help but notice the part he played in this pregnancy. How did he get so lucky? How come he gets to do the fun part, the easy part, and become a father, while I suffer every second of every day in bed?

How is it fair? *Is* it fair? Why did God make it this way?

Was this a punishment?

I had hours upon hours and days upon being stuck inside, living in a new state, having no friends, no car, staring at the wall and wondering why I had to go through this to bring a child here.

Every time I saw my husband eat a meal that used to be delicious to me—that I now couldn't even smell from across the room without throwing up—I would feel angry.

And I didn't know who to direct that anger to.

Was he just not supposed to eat?

Was he supposed to apologize? He often did.

But what could he do to fix it?

So I directed my anger at God. God made it this way. God gave men the easier job—not just easier but fun!

And He gave women the painful part.

Why would He do that to His daughters? Did He love us less? It kind of seemed like He did when I felt so sick and alone.

> Women were given more restrictions and boundaries in religion.

> In some religions, only women had to be covered.

> For centuries, women had less freedom, fewer rights, less safety, less say, less power in the world.

And I thought maybe God made it this way.

And it hurt to my core.

God must be a singular man who gives more to men.

That must be it.

Of course He would have men take on the role of provider, which sounds noble until you realize they get paid for all their efforts. They get *rewarded* for the work they do.

That would be nice, I thought many times.

As I was growing up, I had loved to pray to this Father in the sky, this man I was taught to love but also to serve, and most importantly to please and be perfect for.

I said the words, "Dear Heavenly Father," my whole life and felt good with that. I thought that's all there was: a Father who made all His children that are here on the earth.

And there I was in my suffering in pregnancy, trying to create life— one life—through

>9 months of pure agony,

>9 months of pain,

>depression,

>loneliness.

I had never felt so alone. I had never felt like God didn't love me, until then.

How *could* He love me? How could He send me here to do *this*.

How could He ask me to suffer every minute of every day for nine months—not just once but three times? All while my husband carried on with his normal life, gaining a whole family while he kept his job, health, sleep, workout routine, diet, and all his sanity. And don't get me wrong, he hated this for me; we both did. But how do you solve it? How do you make it fair?

I didn't want to pray to a Father anymore, to someone who never went through what I was going through, who couldn't really understand, just as my husband will never be able to understand, what it is like to carry children and give up so much.

How could He understand this pain? How could He know what it feels like to be pregnant or to be a woman?

No matter what I tried to express in my prayers, it all just felt empty—praying to a man that doesn't suffer at all to create life, yet gets all the glory of it.

All of the glory.

We say things like, "We are all His children." "He loves us." "He created us all."

Every time I would sit in church with my big huge belly, trying to not throw up for the 9,000th time, wishing I were dead while creating a new life, I would hear these words over and over from the pulpit the words I had heard my whole life from the time I was a little girl,but I didn't really HEAR them before.

"He created all of us. We are His children."

There I sat feeling a baby kick me in the ribs, sweating through constant nausea for the ninth month straight, counting down minutes for the last 200 days.

And I thought, *if there was a way for my husband to create our children without me doing this, I'd be in! If he could do it by himself some other way, let's do it!*

In my agony, the words from the pulpit hit me differently.

Having a Heavenly Father seemed like enough UNTIL I became a mother.

And if I had to go through what I did to become a mother, who had to go through this to create me?

Was I really just molded from clay? From a man sitting comfortably on a chair, humming along and sculpting me with His hands?

I wished I could sculpt my children out of clay with my hands. That sounded way easier.

Kinda like becoming a father. Easy.

Not knowing I had a Mother in Heaven this whole time hit me like a ton of bricks.

> *How did I not know?*
>
> *How are we all OK coming from a single-parent home?*
>
> *How come we don't notice that we never mention a Mother?*

If She went through what I went through to create me, I'd like to know. If She knows how I feel, I'd like to know.

If someone sacrificed body, mind, and soul to give me life, I'd like to know!

Where is She? Why don't we speak of Her?

And how do we erase the One Who Creates Life?

How do we not see it?

As I look around, I notice that we have always tried to erase women somehow. We cover them, hide them, quiet them, take them less seriously, diminish their work, their sacrifice, their role in creation.

So many babies are born every day that we've gotten used to it. We take it for granted and brush it off as normal. Every pregnancy for me was anything but normal, although every doctor loved to tell me it was. It broke me mentally, physically, emotionally, and spiritually.

The second pregnancy almost killed me.

I remember trying to fold the laundry with a six-month pregnant belly. I couldn't sit or bend comfortably, and every time I bent over to pick up clothes, I would throw up, which I had been doing for six months straight without breaks, no days off, no moments of reprieve. I was beyond over it. I wanted to crawl out of my skin and leave this sick, uncomfortable body. I just wanted to be able to take a full breath, sleep comfortably, and eat a meal without puking.

My body felt like a prison that I needed to escape to survive.

There I was trying to fold everyone's clothes while my family was running and playing and feeling fine. I was so miserable and the end of my pregnancy felt too far away. I felt so miserable that I often dreamed of death.

Death seemed like my only escape from this existence. Death seemed like sweet relief.

I folded those clothes, and the urge to escape this life and this pain grew inside of me like a wave building. It got to the point where I couldn't resist it.

I dropped the clothes and ran to the banister to leap over it, hoping I could just fall to my death and be done with all of this.

I was halfway over the railing when my husband walked by. He leaped forward and grabbed me.

He was in shock. I was in shock.

It was like I had blacked out. I didn't feel like it was a conscious decision I had made. It felt like a moment of pure survival instinct where death seemed like survival.

No one knew I was feeling this way because, of course, as a woman, you don't show the unpretty, unflattering emotions. You don't want to be a burden to anyone, so you just smile and say, "I'm fine" when people ask how you are doing, even though none of it feels fine, and you want to crawl out of your own skin.

"I'm fine" has become the most common and untrue sentence we utter as humans.

How often do you feel totally "fine," with nothing unsettling on your mind, no worries sitting in your stomach, nothing to be anxious about, nothing to do that seems daunting or stressful? Just fine, fine, fine.

It's usually a lie, but we all say it, and we all believe it. And so many people don't get the help or attention they need for fear of what people will think if they aren't "fine."

I didn't end up dying that day, which meant I had to keep living in my sick body. Keep throwing up. Keep getting bigger and more and more uncomfortable

And feeling more and more angry and disconnected with God.

No matter how many times my brain tried to figure out why God made it this way, I couldn't find a satisfying answer.

I couldn't stand the thought of creating all these children forever and ever this way, and them never knowing I did:

> being in Heaven—a mother, a creator, the giver of life—

> and being unknown, unheard of, unmentioned,

> nameless and faceless to my children

> after I did all the work to create them.

No one could love them more than I could. I knew them. My very blood, tissue, hormones, heartbeat, breath gave them life.

My heart created their hearts,

> my breath, their breath.

Nothing about this seemed just "normal" to me.

Not to me, who almost lost my life to create my children.

And no one could really help me feel better. No one could carry this child inside me when it felt too hard or too heavy. There was no relief for nine months.

Nine!

Almost a full year of having to survive this every day, knowing that the relief was so far away, too far away.

I would often feel so angry that women are somehow considered the weaker of the sexes,

> less strong,
> less capable,
> less valuable in society.

All of the words I had heard my whole life about how girls were fragile, emotional, and dramatic would ring through my head as I lived in exquisite pain and discomfort building a human life, as I birthed three babies through some of the highest pain a human can endure— noticing how incredibly strong, brave, and resilient that was.

And how many women do this more than once knowing how painful it is?

It is the most brave!

So when I hear so many women around me speak about how they are "just" a mom, they don't really do much, they are just messy and scattered, trying to keep up with life, not doing everything perfectly . . .

I want to yell,

NO MORE OF THIS!

No more women creating life and thinking they are not enough.

No more second-guessing our worth and value in this world.

We *are* the world!

We have created the whole world!

And if the world won't see it, I ask you to see it!

See you!

Recognize what you are, who you are, and what you create.

It is everything

because without mothers, we have nothing.

We don't have humans on the planet.

And we don't even have a planet, for it is Mother Earth.

Everything ceases to exist without women. Everything.

Without women going through the sacrifice of pregnancy, the incredible pain of birth, and then giving up so much of their life to protect, raise, nurture, and love those children,

> we lose all other creations.

Without her, no one lives to create.

She cannot be erased.

No.

You cannot be erased.

Maybe the world has tried to erase Her.

But we cannot, for She is always there.

May you never forget that the power that lives within Her resides within you. May you never again doubt the worth that pulses through your very veins.

For you have created life.

And that is the most worthy cause of all.

Section 3

WHY WOMEN FEEL THEY'RE NOT ENOUGH

WOMEN OFTEN NEGLECT THEIR OWN NEEDS, LEADING TO A CYCLE OF SELF-DEPLETION AND FEELINGS OF UNWORTHINESS.

Chapter 13

THE GOD WE NEVER KNEW

To work without pay as a mother is one thing. But mothers often work without acknowledgment or praise, without seeing anything they do stay done, having no finish line to cross at the end of the day, month or year because there is always more to do, more to solve, and endless needs to take care of. Doing this without any awards, bonuses, or paychecks pushes the body, mind, and nervous system to its limits daily.

I often wonder if this is why we don't speak of or worship a Divine Mother—because, in society, we often fail to acknowledge or praise mothers. The role and work of a mother has never been seen as the ultimate symbol of success or worthy of accolades. We casually dismiss it with phrases like, "She's just a stay-at-home mom." Our minds have been conditioned to expect women to work for free, without recognition, without support or help, and to assume they should find joy in this work without ever needing anything in return.

We must assume the Divine Mother operates this way as well, seeing Her as *just* a Mom working tirelessly behind the scenes, unnoticed and unacknowledged. As Her children, we, too, are used to having everything we need each day—the warmth of the sun, moonlight at night, food that grows, and rain that falls—living in the beauty and order She provides, yet we fail to recognize the One Who Sustains It

All. Like all mothers, She continues to care for everything, **even when no one notices.**

Acknowledging Her for all that She creates would break our social norms about how we see mothers and what they do.

As a mother, everything you clean gets dirty, everything you put away ends up back on the floor, everything you organize becomes chaos, every tantrum you resolve leads to another. Every shoe you find is another lost. Every diaper you change comes with more dirty ones.

> There are no finish lines.
> There is no perfect.
> There is no "it's all done."
> There is no end in sight.

This type of work is extremely taxing on the nervous system, brain, body, and emotional well-being because it is constant, often unfulfilling, chaotic, loud, and messy—all things that cause stress and overwhelm in the brain and body. And mothers show up for it everyday.

I know many women, myself included, that believe they are supposed to make everyone comfortable and only speak about things that don't rock the boat. Keep it pretty, easy, and enjoyable for everyone.

That is not this book.

This book will rock the boat. This book will change the way you've always thought about yourself, God, and love. I hope it can heal all those inner thoughts and feelings that ever hold you back, keep you small, and tell you that you are not enough. To heal we must examine the thoughts that race through your mind, the patterns that you have believed about yourself, the reasons you feel less than enough, because when you know why you feel that way and can separate the lies from the truth, your brain will finally let go and change the pattern to create something new.

Throughout time people have given worth and value to things by just deciding what value they *think* it has.

And then we all roll with it.

A coin, dollar, diamond, car, or house—once upon a time someone looked at these objects, made up a price, and gave them a certain value.

This is what brains are good at. Our brains use evidence they can see to measure or define things. So they look at something or someone and guess, assume, and then decide the value they hold.

If we look to our brains or anyone else's to decide our worth or value, that value will be wrong.

We are so vast, expansive, divine, and everlasting.

No brain can understand nor contain our value. We can't weigh and measure it like we do all other things.

As women, we spend so much time trying to weigh and measure our worth.

Our brains get really creative at this.

- numbers on scales
- body fat percentages
- age
- height
- amount of wrinkles
- size of clothes

You name it, we are constantly trying to quantify our value and then compare it to others

>   as if we can add, subtract, and figure out who is the perfect equation.

And as soon as we think we've figured out what a perfect woman should look and act like,

>   *the world changes it!*

Society loves to tell women who they should be, how they should look, what they should and shouldn't say and how they should say it, even how to feel and not to feel.

And we blindly follow. We follow as if our worth depends on it, because we are told it does.

Curvy women were once seen as more desirable and valued—when it was challenging to achieve that figure due to lifestyle and diet. Once that became easier, the preference shifted to thinness. The notion is that whatever comes naturally is considered wrong, and beauty is expected to look like it requires significant effort. Society has created countless molds for what is deemed valuable, and we exhaust ourselves trying to fit into them, never feeling enough as we are.

And instead of pausing to see if any of that feels true to us, we just drink it in and believe it.

Like a game, the world changes the mold constantly, and we all jump in like sharks in a feeding frenzy trying to fit in it,

>   squeezing,

>>   starving,

>>>   conforming,

>>>>   and breaking, to fit into the mold.

The mirror that women are looking into for their value isn't a reflection of who they are, it's who the world wants them to be.

The more they can conform to match that reflection, the more valuable they believe they are in the world.

I've seen many women who have believed that men have the power to give and take their worth, that men ultimately get to decide what they should look like and how they should act. And when a woman gets married, she tries to keep her husband happy by following his rules and expectations for what he wants her to be

> as if her value comes from his approval and his desire to keep her.

This is why it can be so incredibly difficult for women to ever relax into themselves, to ever stop worrying about what everyone thinks of them. And to ever stop doing, proving, and pleasing.

Because women think their value is in other people's comfort and pleasure.

Women shut down their own needs to ensure everyone's needs are met.

Perhaps this is why women hesitate to speak of a Divine Mother, fearing that it might overshadow Heavenly Father. They worry He won't feel needed or that He'll be left out and viewed as less important. Maybe they fear He will be angry or disappointed, much like they've experienced with their fathers or husbands.

And maybe we think He needs the praise and worship to feel loved, but She doesn't. She is fine just making sure we all have everything we need without acknowledgment, just like we as women try to be fine without it.

We are so good at going without.

And the more we go without, the more righteous, strong, and resilient we think we are.

We have tied our worth to being able to survive with less.

We have tied our worth to trying to prove we don't have needs.

We are fine as long as everyone else has what they need.

So we project this onto Heaven, thinking our Divine Mother is the same,

> **imagining She is somewhere behind the scenes**
> **saying that She is fine,**
> **giving the stage to Her husband, letting Him have**
> **all the praise and glory for work She has done,**
>> **creations She has made,**
>> **beauty She has curated,**
>> **life She has birthed,**
>> **love She has shown,**
>> **miracles She performs daily,**
>> **comfort She gives constantly,**
>> **worry She carries.**
> **And just like our own children, we don't notice the**
> **work She does.**

Just like us as mothers, She takes care of the things we need: water, air, food, shelter, sun, nature—all giving life to us every day.

She doesn't let us go without, just like we don't let our kids go without, making sure they have enough of what they need to stay healthy, have opportunities, feel safe, learn, and grow.

Ever watching, sacrificing, and holding our little ones.

And so does She

even if we don't notice Her.

As I write these very words, my people-pleasing self can't help but think of whoever might be reading this sweating, clenching their jaws, and feeling awkward.

I think about how taboo it is for me to say this, how I'm breaking some rule, worried I'm offending Heavenly Father, and I'm going to get punished.

Worried that I'm taking away something from Him by speaking of Her.

But I believe change happens when people speak about what might be taboo.

It was taboo for Martin Luther King, Jr. to speak about black and white people being equal—playing together, sitting together, and working together.

It was taboo in Jesus's time for Him to heal a leper; to touch a woman with an issue of blood; to speak to people who believed differently; to minister with people who had sinned; to perform miracles for those who were unclean and didn't follow the rules; to have imperfect apostles who constantly doubted and made mistakes. Jesus came to this earth and broke the rules of *who* could be helped, sat with, forgiven, blessed, and healed.

It was all taboo. It made people uncomfortable.

They thought He was doing it *all* wrong, and they were angry.

But Jesus continued to speak of love for all, spending time with outcasts, preaching that all are divine and more than enough—**worth His time, worth His mercy, worth His touch and grace—that no one was above or more deserving than another.**

His message changed the world and made more room for everyone, instead of dividing and making one better than the other.

And so it is my desire with this book to speak of the unspoken: to give praise to our Mother too; to believe She took a great role and part in our creation—not only of all of us but of this earth as well. The beauty and the magic of this earth has Her in it and through it.

She is allowed to be thought of, imagined, and heard in our hearts too.

And I believe that when She is,

> hearts will be healed in new ways,
> love will expand,
> and as women, we will come to know ourselves more deeply
> and in a more
> abundant, divine way.

We will have a Godly prototype that looks like us, a Mother like we are mothers, a Woman like we are women.

A God in our image too.

A God who knows how you feel in only the ways a woman can know. A God that understands a woman's brain, a woman's hormones, a woman's body, a woman's worries, and her strength, resilience, and love.

A God who carries Her child in Her heart all day long, watching, protecting, and caring for their needs.

A God who knows what it is like to be a woman and a mother because She is one.

I believe this alone would have the greatest impact on women and how they think of themselves.

When I started this book, I wanted to help women finally let go of the belief that they are not good enough, the belief that they are only a body, size, and shape, that they are someone who serves and supports only. I wanted to help them know, down to their cells, that they aren't too emotional or weak but are women of immense worth

just like God,

that their value cannot be measured with any measurement of the mind,

and neither can Hers.

As I prayed for guidance on what to write, I was open to whatever message God wanted to give me. I didn't have a prewritten book or clear idea of what I wanted to say. I simply asked God to write through me. My mind went quiet, and these words flowed like a river through my hands. They are not my words, they are not from my mind or what I know from my own experience.

I believe they are from Her:

She is there, and we are like Her, and through Her we will be filled with a deep knowing of who we are. We won't have to keep trying to measure ourselves against everyone else, trying to fit in all the molds or beg someone to want us.

Our value is our own; it is given perfectly. There is nothing we can do or not do to lessen it.

If we want to know who we really are, we need to know who we came from: a Father and Mother God so vast, so loving, so divine that no human brain can grasp the grandeur of who we are.

We've always been free and powerful. We've always had a choice, but so often it's forgotten.

We were never actually small or inadequate.

We JUST BELIEVED we were.

We have believed what we have been told.

*But as we get to know Her, we will remember **the truth of who we are.***

Chapter 14

THE BUCKET

"Nothing outside of us is going to change how we feel inside of us."[2]

—Joe Dispenza

Imagine everything you want to be and feel as a large bucket within you—your "self-worth bucket." We all have this internal bucket of needs, and we all desire for it to be filled.

But we were taught that only others can fill it—those around us, those outside of ourselves. This lesson came in many forms as we grew up. We were told that we hurt others' feelings and they hurt ours; that we should "make" people happy, just as others should "make" us happy. We believed we were responsible for everyone's emotions and expected them to manage ours in return. This leads to pain for everyone, as we feel we have no control over or responsibility for the feelings we so desperately desire. We exhaust ourselves trying to manage everyone's emotions, leaving us all frustrated, powerless,

---

[2] Joe Dispenza, "Stories of Transformation - Chris," recorded at Cancun Weeklong Advanced Retreat, 2018, distributed on YouTube August 9, 2018, quote found at 8:22–8:26 on YouTube video, https://www.youtube.com/watch?v=YZliHRK16wk.

resentful, and angry—needing something we can't supply ourselves with while trying to offer feelings to those who won't accept them.

It's as if we were taught that we were born with an empty bucket and that the only way to fill it is through others' approval. This desperation for approval becomes overwhelming because we believe it's the sole path to feeling worthy, valuable, and enough.

The brain is constantly working to meet its needs and "fill the bucket" both physically and emotionally—this is its primary function. It believes that survival depends on safety, connection, love, value, and praise, all of which it assumes must come from others. This leads to feelings of scarcity, fear, and desperation. We find ourselves willing to do almost anything to be liked, thinking it will affirm our sense of safety, worthiness, love, and value.

We do this over and over as we grow,

> *seeking compliments, attention, being included by others, as if they are the only*
>
> *ones that can fill us.*

You allow little drops to be added when people notice you and give you a compliment here and there, **but *only if you believe* those compliments about you are true.**

Needing others to fill your bucket can create a life that feels like you are breathing through a straw. There's some air to breathe, but it never feels like quite enough. Some people seem to get it right and you feel good enough for a moment, and others seem to drill holes in the bottom of your bucket leaving you hurt and angry. This puts the body into a state of constant scarcity and desperation, gasping for more air.

Many of us didn't give much thought to the beliefs we held about ourselves and actively avoided thinking positively about ourselves, fearing we'd come across as prideful or conceited for believing we're amazing, right? Heaven forbid we actually think we're incredible— that's almost worse than feeling like we're not good enough!

We all know it's super charming to think less of ourselves because that's humble, right? It's just so endearing and meek.

No, it's not!

Over time, your brain absorbs the thoughts you've been told and mixes in its own, making them more persistent. Why do certain thoughts stick more than others? Because they're the ones we choose to *believe*.

It's not the thought that hurts us, it's our belief in it.

No one told you that you were the one drilling the holes in the bottom of your bucket.

You drill holes with your own thoughts and beliefs about yourself, not the thoughts and beliefs others have about you.

If you have brown hair and someone comes up to you and says, "I don't like your blue hair" would you immediately be like, "Oh no! I have ugly blue hair!" when you know your hair has always been brown? Would you just so quickly believe it was now blue and ugly? Or would you pause for a minute and question that, and maybe even think that person should get their eyes checked? You would question their thought before you would consider that your hair was blue because you *know* what color your hair is. You don't leave it up for debate, and you don't walk around unsure of it.

You might be confused, but you wouldn't be devastated. You would leave their blue hair comment behind and carry on with your day.

This sounds simple, but it's SO powerful for you to remember.

Because the same is true with ANYTHING someone says to you about who you are. There's no way to stop people from having all kinds of thoughts about you. They are going to. It's how brains work; it's what they do.

But it doesn't have to *mean* anything about you.

"According to research, the average person has approximately 60,000 thoughts per day. But what is truly concerning is that 75% of these thoughts are negative, and 95% are repetitive."[3]

Our brains think thousands of thoughts a day and most are negative and repetitive. *These* **are the thoughts that generate your feelings**, not the thoughts other people might have about you.

When you soak in other people's opinions and assumptions about who you are, you will get confused and lost. You'll exhaust yourself trying to get compliments and assurance about yourself.

As if everyone gets to decide.

When you don't know that your thoughts and beliefs are the only ones that hurt you, you allow anything in. You don't stand guard and protect what you know is true about you. And it becomes so easy to

---

[3] Sandy Loder, "The Impact of 45,000 Negative Thoughts," *Peak Dynamics*, March 10, 2023, https://insights.peak-dynamics.net/post/102ia4i/the-impact-of-45-000-negative-thoughts.

doubt yourself and spin in the lies like an endless loop that circles around and around.

When you doubt your worth constantly, you are drilling holes in the bottom of your bucket, holes that no one else can fill.

When you dwell in self-doubt and self-criticism and someone tells you, "Wow, you're amazing," that compliment will slip straight down and out through the holes at the bottom of your bucket. That compliment won't hold true for you, not because it isn't true but because you've been building and building evidence over too many years of all that is wrong with you, all the ways you mess up, all the things you do wrong . . . drilling more and more holes. So when people say nice things, those thoughts don't hold

because you won't let them.

You just disagree and say things like,

"Oh, no I'm not!"

"Ugh, if you only knew the real me, you wouldn't say that!"

Or if someone says, "You're so beautiful," you'll reply,

"Oh my! You should see me in the morning!"

"You need to get your eyes checked!"

We spend so much of our life chasing compliments, trying to get people to tell us we are good enough and worthy of their time. We've given power to everyone outside of ourselves and then drilled so many holes with our own limiting beliefs that over time *nothing good about us seems true.*

All the compliments feel like lies.

And all the lies feel like the truth.

I've had many clients actively work to reject compliments, argue for their limitations, and try to convince me of and prove all the reasons no one loves them, or all the reasons they can't be successful.

And I see it.

I know it.

Because I have been there.

I brought these beliefs into my marriage, thinking I was only loved for what I did, not for who I was. I maintained an immaculate little house, keeping everything in order. I tried to be constantly happy and agreeable, as I had always done, convinced that love was a transaction based on the value I provided. Whenever conflict arose in my marriage, I feared his love would start to decrease.

Just a month or two into our marriage, my husband and I had a disagreement. We weren't yelling or angry, just trying to understand each other's perspectives. When I saw the frustration on his face, I immediately thought it was my fault. Throughout my life, I had heard countless stories of husbands leaving their wives for various reasons—often because they felt frustrated, unsatisfied, lonely, or simply annoyed. They believed their wives weren't "making" them feel as they wanted, or they thought she was too difficult, or she didn't give them enough attention, or they simply found someone better. This is the story of many of my ancestors, so witnessing my husband's frustration over something I did or said was terrifying. I remember hiding behind the bed, not knowing what to do, waiting for him to just change his mind and leave. He wasn't happy, and I blamed myself, believing he no longer loved me. To me, love was an equation—it was all about actions and pleasing people—and in that moment, I felt I was doing none of that.

I don't even remember what we were arguing about, but I'll never forget the fear that I had lost my husband's love over something so insignificant, all because I disagreed and didn't feel perfect. I remember him standing in the doorway while I hid behind the bed, apologizing to him. He didn't know why I was so scared, and he wasn't even angry, just annoyed. To him it was just a simple conversation. He knew he loved me the same. But to me, love had to be constantly earned and "enough" for someone. He was gentle and he reassured me that his love is constant and that I don't have to agree with him to be loved. He didn't believe love was conditional like I did.

I couldn't understand how someone could love me unconditionally.

When we doubt love and refuse to let it in, as I did, it's like living under a dark cloud—so familiar that we hardly notice it. The shadow feels like home. We've accumulated so much evidence that we are not good enough to be loved that we've come to live under a shroud of lies. This cloud has blocked out the truth and light for so long that we don't know how to exist without it.

If someone tries to love us, we don't trust it. Sometimes we even get angry. "Why are you trying to tell me I'm beautiful, amazing, and capable? Stop it. It's not true, you don't know what you're talking about," you might say.

We have drained ourselves for so long and carried emptiness for years. The darkness is the truest thing we know. And if light comes in, we run and hide. We think we aren't allowed to feel its warmth. It's so uncomfortable it burns. And we scurry back under our dark cloud where we think we belong,

> wishing someone would save us from ourselves, believing, like we always have, that someone else has the answers. If someone just loved us, then we could be filled.

But with all the holes in the bottom of your bucket, no amount of someone else's love for you will hold.

You are the only person that has the power to drill holes, mend holes, and fill or drain your bucket of self-worth.

This is the best news ever

> because you don't have to chase after or depend on others to perfectly meet your needs or say all the words you long to hear.

You can leave people as they are and give yourself what you need. It's the surest way to receive it.

My husband can tell you that I am not even close to being the same person as that young newlywed girl I was years ago, not because he loves me more or any differently—I can't know how much he loves me, *that is only for him to know*—**but now I love me,** *so his love is extra.* Love isn't scarce anymore, and I don't try to earn it from others.

I have worked to patch the holes in my own bucket with the kind of love I now understand as a mother: unconditional, free, and full of grace. I fill the bucket and let it overflow onto people around me, not needing their approval, not needing their love because my bucket is already full. I am enough for me.

Seeing my own self as worthy, lovable, and enough has allowed me to connect with so many people. They can feel safe around me because I don't need *them* to change for *me* to feel better about myself. I can listen to what they are saying without wondering if they like me; I can simply focus on liking them.

This is the freedom I help many women cultivate in my coaching program. I empower women to transform painful relationships, improve communication, and increase their influence within their marriages and families. I help women navigate leaving abusive relationships and building healthier, happier ones. I guide mothers to become the parents they aspire to be, creating space for answers they didn't know they had, and empowering them to craft their lives with purpose and intention. My clients have launched businesses they once only dreamed of and found love they never imagined possible.

This is the legacy I want to leave for women. I believe when women feel more than enough, already worthy, and completely lovable **they change the whole world.** They stop cycles of abuse, and they create incredible impact.

Scan this code for details about my women's group coaching program. Join us weekly on Zoom, where coaching, community, and connection come together in a supportive space. If you're ready to learn alongside other inspiring women and create lasting change in your life, I invite you to be a part of the transformative journey. Discover the power within and step into a future filled with possibility!

This is your permission to stop drilling holes in the bottom of your bucket, hoping someone will come and love you enough to fill the holes in. Even if someone came and loved you perfectly, you wouldn't trust it if you don't *believe* you are lovable. You have everything you need **right now** to be loved. You don't need to be different or better in any way. I promise all you need to do to feel loved is to believe you are worthy of it and that it is always yours to generate for yourself and others. You don't have to earn it, buy it, beg for it, and run from it. Patch the holes, and fill your bucket with what you like about yourself first before you try to get anyone else to like you.

Chapter 15

THE BRAIN

I believe we existed before coming to earth, before our bodies were formed. Each of us has a soul—a deep-seated knowing within us. Our soul understands far more than our human brain, having existed for much longer. It recognizes the truth. In contrast, our human brain struggles to grasp perfect truth. Our bodies serve as a home for our souls on earth, containing the vast, expansive being within us that comprehends worlds, experiences space and light, and understands creation on a grand scale. This soul was given a body and a brain—a brain to sustain life and a body to house the soul, allowing it to fully experience human life, feeling, and energy.

We were given a body that allows our soul to experience the full range of emotions—from the warmth of love to the depths of grief and loneliness. This body is a precious gift, enabling us to understand others' feelings and build relationships, while the brain ensures our survival by keeping our organs functioning, blood pumping, and lungs breathing

so we can experience it all,

so we can choose

and truly live.

But your brain isn't the teller of truth. Your brain doesn't remember who you were before being in this body. Your brain wasn't there with your soul. Your brain is new. It only knows what you have experienced in the short years you've been alive.

And because your brain wants to keep you safe and alive

> *it worries, it wonders, it doubts and fears.*

It fears all the possible problems,

> *all the possible pain.*

It runs ahead into the future and guesses how it will all go wrong and become dangerous.

It will tell you,

> *you don't know what you are doing;*
> *you are going to fail;*
> *nobody likes you;*
> *you're not good enough;*
> *this won't work.*

You hear these thoughts often, so often **that you start to believe them.** They start to feel so familiar, and over time they become your truth.

This becomes the filter through which you see yourself and the world.

You find yourself often feeling

> *afraid,*
> *anxious,*
> *uncertain,*
> *and confused.*

And it makes sense to feel that way when you believe the fears and lies your brain tells you.

Your brain doesn't want to hurt you. It really doesn't. It just wants to keep your body alive!

That's its job.

To the brain you are only your body—fragile and breakable—and it wants to protect you, so it assumes everything is going to hurt you.

> *People could hurt you, so don't go to that social gathering.*
> *Places could hurt you, so don't travel and explore.*
> *Love could hurt you, so close your heart, build walls, and don't*
> *let people in.*
> *Relationships could hurt you, so people please, pretend, and assume you will be rejected.*
> *Your ideas could fail, so don't dream, don't create, and don't try.*

When we believe the brain, we stay small because we *believe* we are small.

We fixate on what we *can't* do or be.

But you are not your brain, and you are not your body.

You *have* a brain and you *have* a body.

But you are *more* than that.

The brain is a gift to your vast soul that needs a home for now, that needs safety and survival, *for now.*

Your soul needs to experience humanness.

But you are not fragile, or small, or not enough.

Anytime you believe you are limited, less than someone else, or not capable enough for your dreams, wants, or desires—**it's a lie.**

How do you know lies from truth?

Lies feel dark, scarce, confusing, and heavy **because they are not the truth about you.**

Truth *feels* like the opposite of lies.

It feels warm, vast, abundant, safe, fun, clear, and hopeful.

Your brain won't always give you the truth about who you are. It doesn't really know.

To find the truth about you, you have to look to your soul—

> **a soul that knows more because it has existed longer.**

If you think you are not good enough, your brain will look for evidence that it's true.

That's what brains are made to do:

> look for evidence of its thinking.

So the brain goes to work looking, listening, searching, and taking note of anything and everything that proves you're not good enough.

But not good enough for what?

Not good enough for whom?

Your brain doesn't stop to answer these questions. *It just runs as fast as it can to gather proof.*

This is one of the main reasons women feel they are not enough: the brain is ALWAYS searching for WHY they are not enough. The brain is on the hunt . . . all day . . . every day . . . to find the proof of your "not enoughness,"

- noticing all the times you aren't invited instead of all the times you are,
- focusing on the people who don't like you, instead of those that do

Say you're out with your friends, and everyone is talking about their week, their day, how their vacation went, what has been hard lately, etc.

You chime in. You start talking about your day or week, and you get interrupted by someone; they remember something fun they wanted to share, or something you said sparked an idea for them.

They start talking without even realizing you were in the middle of your story. You stop. You say, "It's fine."

And your brain takes note.

It must be because you're not good enough to entertain them, not interesting enough for them to hear you.

So you shut down, and you get quiet.

There it is again . . . proof. A little more proof.

> *If you were good enough, people would listen, your brain thinks.*

Then there are moments when you're surrounded by kids, cooking dinner while hurrying them to the bathroom, trying to recall their football practice time, realizing you forgot to get the gift for their friend's birthday party, and dealing with toddlers melting down over the bumps in their socks—all while the dinner burns on the stove.

You all sit down to dinner just to hear your toddler say, "I hate this food, it's gross. You're the worst mommy."

And your brain picks it up and stores it in the pile of evidence.

> *I'm not good enough, or else I could handle all of this.*
> *I can't even make dinner without messing it up.*
> *How do other moms do it?*

So you try harder. "Just be more perfect," your brain tells you, "then maybe we could be good enough."

You look forward to Sunday, thinking you'll go to church and feel enough. Maybe that's where you'll find it. *They talk about Jesus there, so it has to be there, right!?*

You wake up Sunday morning, try to get the kids bathed and ready in their Sunday best. They get in the tub. The youngest gets soap in her eyes. The others are splashing you as you try to wash their hair.

You can't find their church pants, and once you do they don't like how they fit, so as soon as they are dressed and you move on to help the other child, the first one is undressed again.

You circle back, trying to find pants he will wear; everything is too long, or too short, not the right pockets or color.

So you give up and put him in sweatpants.

You go to get yourself in the shower with minutes to spare, everyone asking you questions and bombarding you while you have soap in your own eyes.

> "What should I eat for breakfast?"
> "I can't find my socks."
> "We are going to be late."

You rush out of the shower, searching for a dress that fits a body that has changed sizes countless times since bringing these little ones into the world. Nothing feels right—it's either too tight and restricting your breath, too short, or the zipper won't budge.

So you throw on an old maternity dress even though you're not pregnant, but it fits and it's comfortable.

You pull your hair into a wet bun and try to find everyone's missing shoes.

You get to church looking for relief for your not-enoughness. *Tell me stories of Jesus. Tell me I'm worthy, please.*

And you get there late. Someone has to pee. So you run them to the bathroom, only for them not to make it.

They pee down their leg and yours, right into your shoe.

Back home you walk, with one squishy, pee-filled shoe and one crying toddler.

What pants will you put them in now?

You feel defeated.

You believe everyone else was at church on time, perfectly showered, hair blown dry and curled.

How do they do it?

Then your brain assumes the answer, as usual: *They must be better than me. What is wrong with me? I'm such a hot mess.*

By the time you make it back to church, you've missed most of it. *Again.* This isn't the first time, and you know it won't be the last.

Something must be wrong with you—just you. Not anyone else.

They have it all together; they do it better, you think. *They are never late. Their kids don't complain, pee their pants, or run around screaming like wild monkeys.* Just yours do that, because of you. If you could just be a better mom, maybe your kids would behave like their kids.

From burnt dinners, missed meetings, mess ups, sticky floors, unfolded laundry, and imperfect kids, you have all the evidence you need to believe you're just broken, unworthy, unlovable, and not good enough.

As if any of that *means* anything about you.

But we are conditioned to think that everything outside of ourselves determines our value and is proof of our worthiness and capability. We are taught and trained that our value is in what we accomplish, earn, and achieve. It needs to be proven but also recognized *by others* as good enough.

We want to believe we are inherently valuable and worthy. But we never hear or see evidence of that. We don't give or receive praise for just existing, for having a range of human emotion, for trying and failing or for not trying at all. We don't get praised for waking up and doing the day. That's just expected. We typically only get praised when we are winning awards, beating our opponent, not crying, not struggling, not missing, or not messing up.

And so our brain is wired to seek those things as if they our only way to acceptance: needing to prove more and more that we are worthy of love; living for achievements; pushing ourselves and our children to exhaustion trying to win, produce, achieve, and accomplish because we fear that if we don't, we will be worthless, unwanted, and rejected.

We fear that if we give or receive praise too easily, then we will be weak. We won't try, we won't work hard or accomplish great things.

We have created a society of exhausted, anxious people who are constantly competing and comparing themselves to others—never feeling enough because there is always someone who is doing more, working harder, making more money, or achieving more success—which creates an insatiable hunger to be more, create more, and have more while never feeling satisfied or happy with what we have or who we are.

When you compare yourself to another person, it shuts you down and kills your magic and your energy.

God did not make you like anyone else. That's obvious to see. No two people are exactly alike because they aren't supposed to be. *You* are not supposed to be like anyone else. When you try to compare yourself to or copy someone, you dissolve the power of your unique gifts, strengths, and purpose. That's why it feels awkward—because it should. Being anyone other than yourself should feel uncomfortable and strange. It's supposed to so you will come back to yourself—like coming home—to what is natural, comfortable, and real.

If we stopped trying to compare, and we just believed we are more than enough as we are . . .

> born with everything we need to succeed in our own way;
> trusting that what comes most natural to us is divine and has purpose, that we don't need to force or pressure ourselves into something that we weren't made for,
> that what flows most naturally and easily is what we will be most successful at;
> trusting ourselves instead of doubting ourselves constantly;
> noticing what we are good at instead of what we lack;
> not seeing ourselves in comparison to others but seeing our unique differences as our strengths . . .

just imagine how we would show up everywhere we went. Imagine the peace, and confidence that comes from knowing that who you are is complete, whole, and worthy no matter what mistakes you make, feelings you feel, or how you compare to others.

This is the freedom you seek. This is what quiets the noisy ache inside. It can and only will be filled by you.

Section 4

EMOTIONS

WHEN YOU BASE YOUR WORTH ON OTHERS' EMOTIONS,
YOU GIVE UP YOUR OWN PEACE.

Chapter 16

EMOTIONS ARE NOT
THE PROBLEM

Women are often labeled as too emotional, as if there's some magical ruler that determines the perfect amount of emotion one should have. Apparently, men have just the right amount, but women have too much, making them appear unfit to make decisions, lead, or be taken seriously, and sometimes women are even regarded as irrational.

The truth is,

emotion is the language of God.

Emotion is one of the main reasons we came to this earth and were given a body—

so we could feel!

Feel it all because that is how we *experience* this life.

Without emotion, *life is hell!*

We wouldn't have desire, motivation, goals, dreams, or relationships without emotion; there would be no need for any of it if we didn't get to experience how it felt.

Emotion is what our brain wants most, actually! It's what motivates us toward anything and everything. It is the fuel source to all of our actions.

Emotion is the body's language—it communicates how we feel and what we need. When danger arises, our emotions rush in and guide us to safety. Emotion lets us know when something is right or wrong for us. It gives us feedback and information. We feel a wide range of different emotions that can either feel pleasant or uncomfortable, but they aren't inherently right or wrong; they simply exist, as we do. When we constantly try to suppress emotion, argue with it, or pretend it isn't there, it leads to pain.

Suppression leads to depression!

Because we are designed to feel, when we try to shove emotion down, pretend it's not there, or constantly argue with it, we will feel even more sad, angry, or depressed.

Everything we desire, pursue, or strive for is motivated by the feeling we believe it will bring us.

Isn't that crazy?!

Think of anything you want . . .

- *money*
- *a dream house*
- *a relationship*
- *children*
- *a new job*
- *a vacation*
- *a million followers*

Why do you want these things?

Try to give a reason without saying how you think you would *feel* if you had them.

It's hard, right?

Think of something you really want right now or in the future.

I want _____ because I would **feel** _____!

You might say having a lot of money would feel *fun, exciting, or fulfilling.* Or maybe you would feel *relieved, safe, or secure.*

If you want a relationship, ask yourself *why?* Do you believe you would feel loved, happy, safe, connected, or excited? **That is why you want it,** *because you desire those feelings.*

Emotion is what we want. We all just want to *feel* something.

AND

> at the same time, we *don't want* to feel all the uncomfortable emotions.

We spend most of our time chasing positive emotions and avoiding negative ones.

> We are all emotional!

And maybe that's the purpose of this human experience. We don't get to take our awards, money, cars, or fame with us when we die. All we get to take with us is our experience, and we can't experience anything without feeling the emotion of it.

What if it was never wrong to feel, to express or show sadness, worry, disappointment, or anger?

What if it was the *most* right thing?

For centuries, people have tried to suppress emotions, believing it is a sign of weakness. Along the way we've become masterful at hiding our emotions in various ways, holding them in until we feel sick, hiding tears like our lives depend on it, avoiding difficult conversations, or masking emotion with dangerous drugs and cheap dopamine—doing all we can to make sure no one knows we feel anything, believing it is better to pretend to be happy than to admit we are sad.

We live in a world where emotionlessness is often equated with strength, bravery, resilience, and trustworthiness. Society tends to celebrate those who hide their emotions, especially the negative ones. We've been conditioned to feel neutral and act like we are "fine" with everything, fearing that showing emotion might cost us the respect of others. We often expect people to function like robots—without highs or lows, without expression, and certainly without tears.

It's no surprise that the most successful companies are those offering an escape from negative emotions through inexpensive, short-lived dopamine hits.

- alcohol
- drugs
- pornography
- video games
- TV and movies
- candy
- prescriptions

Anything to numb our ability to feel is the name of the game.

But as soon as those "drugs" wear off, the feelings rush back like a wave to meet you.

They don't go away for good; you just keep hitting pause over and over again with suppression, dopamine hits, or distractions.

If you have to try so hard to *not* have a feeling, maybe you're *supposed* to have one!

Women were never crazy or too emotional. They had it right all along.

We are supposed to feel deeply. It isn't a weakness, it is our Godlike strength. For without the intensity of our emotion, we would not have the intensity of our love, compassion, empathy, and care. Without the wide range of emotion, mothers wouldn't have the intuition, deep knowing, and understanding of the needs of their children. Because of our emotions we intuitively know how to care for our children so automatically without question.

The truth is, emotions are crucial to our existence, guiding us, connecting us, and creating our experiences. When we realize that we are supposed to have feelings, we allow ourselves to experience life more fully. Expressing our emotions is a sign of strength and authenticity, and it's time we redefine what it means to be strong and brave, no longer linking strength and bravery to being emotionless robots.

As a coach, I've had the privilege of helping countless clients process their emotions, and it's remarkable to see how transformative this practice can be. I've witnessed individuals transition from feeling stuck, overwhelmed, bitter, angry, and hopeless to finding peace, feeling centered, and becoming excited about their future—sometimes in just one session. This change happens so quickly because I provide them with a safe space to express how they feel without fear of judgment. When emotions are allowed to move through and out of the body, it makes room for new, positive emotions to take their place.

When we suppress emotion, we trap the suffering inside, allowing it to build until we eventually snap, lose control, or make decisions that cause further pain. By expressing emotion, we release it from our body, allowing us to find relief.

Imagine if we extended this same compassion and understanding to one another—our friends, coworkers, and neighbors, parents to children, husbands to wives. We would create more safety, connection, influence, and impact in all of our relationships, reducing suffering, mental illness, and even suicide. We wouldn't be emotionally suppressed robots pretending we are fine until we break.

One of the greatest gifts you can offer someone you love is a safe space for them to feel and express their emotions without judgment, shame, ridicule, blame, or dismissal. This openness creates freedom, deeper trust, and genuine connection. Emotion is the universal connector; we all experience it, recognize it, and relate to it. So, don't shut down your emotions or fear them, and don't let them define you.

Remember, how you feel is not who you are! There's no need to criticize or judge yourself for your emotions. Our capacity to feel was given to us with intention, knowing that it would enrich our lives and serve the greater good for us all.

Chapter 17

THE PURPOSE OF EMOTIONS

Emotions are for you. You were designed to have them. This was not a flaw in the make up of who you are. This is your greatest strength and resource.

Why would we get married or have children if we didn't feel anything? It wouldn't make any sense and the brain wouldn't want to expend time or energy on it.

Your brain's primary job is to keep you alive and safe. You need energy to stay alive, so the brain conserves it unless it seems necessary to use it.

As I've talked about, the reason your brain will give precious energy to anything is for how it thinks it will get to feel if it has that thing.

If I came to you and said,

"Hey, do you want children? This is what you will have to do.

- Be pregnant for nine months.
- Gain a lot of weight.
- Feel sick most of the time.
- Give birth for hours in the most intense pain.
- Wake up multiple times through the night for years.

- Take care of their every need when it's most inconvenient for you.
- Have stretch marks, scars, aches, and pains.
- Wipe bums.
- Clean up messes all day.
- Do five times the amount of laundry.
- Eat food they like instead of food you like.
- Walk on Legos and cracker crumbs most of your life.
- Take care of them when they are sick, then you'll get sick."

If you looked at this list using only your brain's logic, and reasoning—*would you be in? Would you think this was a good idea?*

Or would you say, "No way! Why would anyone do that?!"

It makes no sense until I tell you how it *FEELS* to have children.

If after you saw that list, I said,

"But . . .

- you will **feel** the most delicious love you've ever experienced;
- you will **feel** a joy that you didn't know existed before;
- you will smell them and smell heaven;
- when they smile for the first time, you will **feel** a happiness you can't even imagine;
- when they walk for the first time, you will cheer with excitement and **feel** so proud;
- you will never **feel** more alive at times, and in some moments never more significant and loved."

Does it change it at all? Does your brain go from, "No way!" to, "Wait a minute, hmmm. That sounds interesting. It might sound worth it"?

Consider the countless children who have entered this world despite the immense difficulty and pain involved in bringing each one here. No person simply appears; each life arrives through some measure of sacrifice and struggle.

And even after you go through all of that for one child, once you know the emotion, once you feel that love—which at times can be instant—your brain is willing to do it again! Only because of the love, joy, fulfillment, and happiness that little life opened you up to.

Isn't that wild?

If we didn't feel anything, we would never want to take care of little people with endless needs all day. The messes and tantrums—none of it would make any sense at all.

We want the children because of how it *feels* to have them, to love them. It's one of the best—if not *the best*—feelings we can have on this earth: to love a child who doesn't and can't *earn* our intense love.

During pregnancy, we are constantly in some sort of discomfort: nausea, fatigue, aches, sickness. It would make more sense to be angry with that baby for making us so uncomfortable.

But when that child is born, we feel immediate love—the best feeling in the world—born through the most pain we've ever experienced.

And we aren't mad at the baby for our pain, we don't hate the baby because of the agony we endured.

We gave our life to bring them here, and then we spend our lives keeping the baby alive. We give up our own ease, pleasure and comfort for them to have theirs, when they never earned it.

They don't make our lives easier. In many ways, life is much harder. But we do it all because of

love.

That one emotion is the most powerful emotion created, felt, and experienced.

Women go through the most excruciating pain to get to that love, a love that is not earned by their child.

And maybe that is how God loves us too.

So please, never again judge yourself for the emotions you feel! They need no judgment, only grace and understanding. They come to give you insight, discernment, awareness, and experience. And as a woman, you get to experience so much more because you *feel* so much. If you allow these feelings to come and go like waves in the ocean—ebbing and flowing—you will be able to process them more easily, and you will find more safety and trust in yourself as they come, seeing their purpose and letting them pass.

Self-judgment for emotions will only increase the intensity of the emotions. So breathe, relax into them, understand them, and they will let go. I've witnessed it hundreds of times.

Learning how powerful your emotions are, how they impact what you do, how they fuel what you create for your life, and knowing that you have the ability to shift and change your emotions by your thinking is the greatest gift I could give you because it has changed everything in my life.

Chapter 18

MEN AND EMOTIONS

We all have emotions and try all kinds of things to escape the uncomfortable ones. But in this chapter, I want to bring some context to why men seem to struggle more with expressing or allowing their emotions.

I believe with more context comes more compassion.

So I want to shed some light on why I believe men have a hard time with vulnerability and showing emotion, with the hope that we can better understand them and help them navigate emotions with more grace.

In society we treat little girls and little boys differently. We have different rules and expectations for them. We cultivate in them what we believe they need to be.

Little boys have been told that showing emotion is weak. They are often told, *do not be emotional; that's what girls do but not boys.*

When boys are mocked for displaying emotion, their brains quickly associate expressing feelings with pain. They hear insults and are called wuss, sissy, weak, or are told that they are *acting like a girl.*

And when they *don't* show emotion, they are praised. They are told they are strong, brave, tough, fearless, and capable.

We increase what we praise.

Little boys become wired to believe that crying, expressing, feeling nervous, afraid, worried, or anxious means they are bad, weak, and "less of a man." And holding in emotion, not talking about it, lying about it, choking it down, and saying they are fine means they are *manly and strong.*

These boys grow up to be men who are disconnected and detached from their emotions, not realizing emotions are still running their lives below the surface.

Pretending they don't have emotions doesn't make the emotions go away. It just increases every urge for substances, distractions— anything to ensure they don't feel a negative emotion.

This is where the brain can easily become addicted to substances— drugs, pornography, busy-ness, food, screens, etc. The brain wants the fastest way out of negative emotion, and these things flip that switch from negative to positive emotion the fastest. The urge for a substance can feel so intense, as if their life depends on escaping these emotions. It turns into a cycle that can feel impossible to break.

When people believe feeling emotion is dangerous and threatening to their character, every way out of feeling these emotions is consuming.

When they feel a negative emotion . . .

- shame,
- anger,
- sadness,
- loneliness,

- worry.
- anxiety,
- guilt,
- boredom,
- embarrassment . . .

the brain will quickly feel an urge to distract them from that emotion.

If they answer the urge they will feel relief from the emotion for a short time. But once that distraction or dopamine hit wears off, they will be met with the same emotion *and* an added layer of shame for doing something that doesn't align with who they want to be.

Layers of negative emotion start to build, and the urges to escape become more intense, leading to a painful loop that creates so much suffering and addiction.

Addictions are often a result of emotions we aren't willing to feel or understand.

The more we try to outrun emotions, the more pain we will cause ourselves

> **because God never intended us to live a life without feeling.**

When we try to numb ourselves from feeling, we make decisions that create more pain, more problems, and more negative emotion keeping us stuck in a loop:

> Avoiding the emotion → Acting on an Urge → Feeling even worse afterward → Needing to escape again → Avoiding more intense emotions → Choosing more intense distractions
> . . .

This is a loop of destruction and pain.

The secret to ending this loop . . .

is simple.

It's allowing yourself to feel.

If you can sit with a rising emotion and not run from it immediately by scrolling on your phone, binging TV, taking a drug, playing video games, etc., then you will have so much more power and control over your decisions and your results. You will be able to create your life on purpose—you will be able to connect more deeply with those you love, you will be far more satisfied with yourself and the choices you make—because you will be able to choose your life instead of running from it, hiding, masking, feeling numb or ashamed for not being who you want to be.

The Shame Blame Trap

If there was something I could yell from the rooftops that would reach every woman's ear, I would teach them about the shame blame trap so they can know what it is and not let themselves be swept up in someone else's shame loop.

Shame is one of the lowest vibrations we feel in our bodies. It feels terrible. It hurts. So our brain wants the fastest way out of that feeling. A common solution most brains turn to is to blame someone else. Our brain thinks that if it can quickly blame someone else, we will convince them and *ourselves* that it wasn't our fault, hoping to be relieved of the shame.

Because many young boys are told not to feel, they grow up to be men that don't know how to feel and don't feel safe to feel. So their brains find ways to get out of feeling emotions as quickly as possible. One of those ways is to defend themselves, deflect, argue about things they aren't proud of, shut down, or blame someone else for what they did or how they feel.

Shame is one of the most significant wounds men carry. They feel shame for what they've done, what they think, those they've hurt, mistakes they've made, and emotions they feel. Society expects them to be "strong," which often means not showing emotion, not talking about feelings, and not allowing themselves to acknowledge that they even have feelings. This misconception doesn't make them strong; it makes them suffer in silence, becoming more frustrated, resentful, and angry. It leads to headaches, stomachaches, high blood pressure, autoimmune disorders and many other health problems, and an inability to connect with loved ones.

In their desperation for relief, they turn to distractions—phones, TVs, games, gambling, pornography, drugs, and more—seeking brief moments of relief from shame. Yet, when those distractions end, shame only compounds. Confronting their emotions can feel terrifying after a lifetime of suppressing them to avoid appearing weak.

When a man hasn't felt safe to show emotion, he will often have layers of unprocessed emotions under the surface, and at any moment the pressure of all of these emotions can burst unexpectedly like a volcano.

This can look like yelling, arguing, blaming, avoiding, or deflecting.

If he feels shame about something, he will blame someone else for it. This is the shame blame trap. He doesn't know how to process or talk about shame, and his brain thinks blaming it on someone else will relieve him of this painful emotion.

If you are in someone's shame blame trap, see it for what it is, and don't make it mean something about you. It is just the brain's way of trying to escape emotion—not acknowledging it, not talking about it, and making you think *you* did something wrong instead of them.

Their brain is just trying to feel better, and this is the way that seems most efficient.

You can have compassion for the shame or uncomfortable emotion he must feel, but don't pick it up, and don't drink it in.

It's not about you, it's not for you, and you don't need to solve it. You don't need to argue back or defend yourself for something you didn't do. Just see it for what it is, and let it land in front of you.

Here are some options of things you can say when you are noticing your spouse in a shame blame trap:

"You must really be hurting. Let me know if you want to talk about it."

"You must be carrying a lot. It's OK if you need to let it out. If you can be respectful to me as you do, I'm here to listen."

Negative emotion can feel so dangerous and uncomfortable when a man has been told his whole life not to have it.

It doesn't mean YOU are causing his negative emotion.

Because shame is one of the lowest vibrational emotions, as we carry it we create a lot of disease in our bodies. It can make us sick if we hold onto it. So, out of survival, the brain will want to blame the actions we are not proud of on someone else, thinking we will get relief from the pain *if it isn't our fault.*

This is why coaches call it a *shame blame trap*, because it goes in a loop, around and around without any real relief or peace.

You can help by not jumping in the loop and arguing over who did what or trying to defend yourself.

If he is drowning in shame, don't jump in and punch each other in the face by fighting and blaming each other back and forth. Stay outside the pool he is drowning in, trust what you know is true for you, and throw in a rope by letting him know you are here to listen without judgment. You care how he feels. You aren't going to fight. You can be a safe place for him to express himself.

Here are some things you can do to create that safe space for anyone who struggles to express themselves, be vulnerable, or who easily jumps to blame or anger.

- Ask questions about how they feel *without telling them* how they feel.
- Let them know they are allowed to feel however they feel, and you still love them.
- Tell them you want to hear more and won't judge them for how they feel.
- Validate the emotion. You don't have to validate the behavior or reasons.
- Reassure them that feelings don't mean anything about who they are.

Listening without arguing, judging, criticizing, or defending is a powerful way to pull someone out of the shame blame trap and help them break free from the cycle of suppressing and exploding. With support, they can adopt a new mindset that it's safe to feel and express emotion—both positive and negative, comfortable and uncomfortable. Becoming a safe person for someone to process emotion with allows them to release old fearful patterns from childhood.

They need people who can genuinely ask about and listen to how they feel without judgment. And, like everyone else, they need to learn to be gentle with themselves, stop beating themselves up over their feelings, and avoid shaming themselves when emotions aren't all positive.

If we could redefine strength, bravery, and masculinity to include being emotionally aware, expressive, vulnerable, and honest about feelings, we would foster real strength in men.

There would be less suffering, pain, war, divorce, abuse, addiction, and suicide.

Emotion is our most divine gift; it's not the problem. But when we make it a problem, we suffer. In truth, it is the ultimate solution to all our problems.

Chapter 19

EMOTIONAL ADULTHOOD

So many women I have coached are desperately seeking their husband's approval. Each of these women hangs on her husband's every word and command of what he wants from her, then rushes around trying to do everything to his satisfaction, exhausting herself in the process, neglecting herself—not even noticing what *she* desires—just hoping that she can be enough for him, that she can meet his needs and satisfy his desires. Each woman does this in a panic, as if her worth depends on it. She lives in fear that if her husband is unhappy, frustrated, or angry, it MUST be her fault. She must have done something to cause his dissatisfaction.

Because we all know that a woman is responsible for a man's emotions, right?

WRONG!

Why do we keep taking responsibility for something we are not responsible for nor have any control over? If you had control over your husband's emotions, do you think you would EVER choose anger, frustration, sadness, depression, or anxiety?

No!

If *you* create his emotions, why doesn't he feel the way you want him to?

Because you *don't* create his emotions. You can't, even if you try to.

Men are responsible for their own feelings. They always have been, they always will be. And you are responsible for your emotions as well.

This is called **emotional adulthood**:

> taking responsibility for the thoughts that generate your emotions and allowing the other adult to be responsible for their thinking, feeling, and acting as well.

Emotional childhood is thinking we are responsible for everyone's feelings, and everyone is responsible for ours.

Most people never grow and mature into emotional adulthood. They mature mentally, physically, and spiritually, but not emotionally. They carry their emotional childhood into adulthood, which wreaks havoc on their relationships, careers, and ability to live a fulfilling life.

Children think all of their emotions are someone else's fault. They blame others for what they feel and how they act because children don't understand how to be responsible for these things at a young age. They are used to being taken care of and depending on their parents for safety, security, trust, and survival.

As we grow and develop, we learn how to take care of ourselves, we learn how to make decisions, and we learn how to be responsible for our jobs, our children, and the things we own.

But most of us never learn to be responsible for *how we feel,* which keeps us in an emotionally childlike state, believing our spouse, children, boss, friends, and coworkers should give us the feelings we want. This often leaves us angry and frustrated because the brain doesn't think it has control of what it wants to feel.

Every time your husband is feeling a negative emotion, you need to know YOU DID NOT GENERATE THAT FOR HIM. His own thoughts are generating his emotions. And the same goes for women. This is how being human works. We don't hand people feelings. We don't create each other's emotional experiences.

We don't walk around waving magic wands making people feel the feelings we want them to.

Wouldn't that be fun though?!

When we think we are responsible for everyone's feelings—our husband's, our kids', our friends', our neighbors', our sisters', our brothers', our parents'—we don't leave any space for people to feel. We try to control it, talk them out of it, and distract them from it.

And we work tirelessly trying to resolve everyone's emotions, trying to make everyone feel better, which, I understand, *seems like noble work.*

I'm not saying you shouldn't care how people feel.

> You care because you are Godly.
> You care because you love.

So of course you want to fix how they feel, and want to make them feel better.

That is empathy.

But when we run around trying to save everyone from their emotional experiences,

> we lose ourselves.
>> We become controlling,
>>> manipulative,
>>>> angry,
>>>>> resentful.

Women are constantly trying to get their worth from everyone feeling happy.

Your worth has NOTHING to do with anyone's happiness or sadness.

Nothing.

Stop trying to measure your value with everyone's emotional states.

This won't make you less loving.

> It will make you MORE.

I promise.

Trust that we all came here to experience emotion and that this is why we were given bodies—to feel! **Don't argue with it.**

ALLOW IT.

We were never supposed to *just feel happy* here.

Or else we would.

We were never meant to *only feel sadness*.

Or else we would.

We were sent here to feel it all, so we could understand it, so we could discern truth from lies, so we could know what to do and what not do, so we could tell the difference between light and darkness, so we could understand choice and consequence.

> So we could empathize with each other and understand how someone else feels.

> So we could better care for and connect with others.

We actually connect more deeply in pain, sadness, grief, anger, and disappointment . . .

> because it's so human, and we all know how it feels.

It's not your job to make sure no one feels anything. That's not what you came here for.

It's actually the opposite.

You came here to feel, so you could create, express, and impact; so you could bring your light and transmute the darkness in this world. If you didn't feel, you wouldn't care, and you wouldn't create change.

Without feeling, there is no connection.

Without feeling, we don't create anything.

How fun would it be to have robot children?

> Or watch robots play sports?
> Or have a robot for a spouse?
> A robot pet?
> A robot parent?

Robots can be programmed to do anything we want them to do with precision—no mistakes, no emotion, just doing.

> No arguing or tantrums.
> No excuses or fighting.

Robots just do.

It would be fun for about a day, maybe two. And then guess what?

You'd be bored!

> Lonely!
> Disconnected!
> Sad!
> Disappointed!

What?! How could that be?! I thought we wanted everyone to do everything perfectly and feel fine all the time.

But when we remove emotion . . .

we remove

- love,
- connection,
- happiness,
- peace,
- fun,
- variety,
- excitement,
- wonder, and
- joy.

Robots don't feel.

But would that be better? Is that what you really want? A world with robot humans that have no emotion?

No.

Emotion is the purpose.

You don't need to keep everyone happy to be a good mom or to be a worthy woman.

That belief was a lie.

You came here to live, to breathe, to connect, and to feel.

You came exactly as you needed to.

Section 5

TRUTH AND LIES

YOU CAN KNOW IF YOUR THOUGHTS ARE TRUE BY HOW THEY FEEL IN YOUR BODY. BRAINS CAN BELIEVE ANYTHING—LEARN TO TRUST YOUR INTUITION.

Chapter 20

TRUTH AND LIES, BELIEF AND DOUBT

There are many opposing forces we are met with on our journey through life; some work for you while others work against you,

like

belief and doubt.

Many of us have been taught to trust and believe in everybody *but* ourselves, to look to others for who we should be.

To copy and paste.

We often hear correction from so many different voices. And we keep adjusting ourselves to try to fit in all the molds.

If we could just please them all, **we would get it right.**

But is being anyone other than you . . . right?

Why would you be here, then?

Anytime you believe you're supposed to be someone else,

it's a lie,
it limits you.

The force that works against you is doubt.

Doubt is like a heavy, dark wave that rolls in when you least expect it. **It comes when you're on the edge of belief.**

It can roll in like a thick wave, sweeping you up, spinning you around with all kinds of fear, what ifs—*how it could all go wrong.* You spin in this wave, holding your breath, waiting for someone to come, waiting for rescue, because it can feel like death.

It fills your lungs, it clamps your throat. It's hard to speak or even believe anything could be good, true, easy, or clear again.

It's easy for our brains to doubt. It doesn't take effort and energy to doubt. We can slip right into it without trying, without wanting to.

The lies that doubt tells can seem so real and so true to our human minds because our brains are designed to protect us from danger. So danger is what the brain looks for. It is scanning for it all the time . . .

> *thus creating it, unintentionally.*

Doubt can seem far more true than belief,

> *especially when it's about ourselves.*

I have sat with countless clients from ages ten to seventy-five, and I have listened to them express their doubts, fears, and worries. They are filled with anxiety. *And it makes sense*

> **because when we believe the doubt, our bodies fill with stress and anxiety.**

The anxiety is like the red indicator light on your car dashboard that warns you that something is off. Something needs attention, something needs to change for your car to run smoothly.

When we see that red light pop up on our cars, we may feel inconvenienced, but we don't blame the light. We aren't angry at the light for bringing our awareness to something that needs to be fixed.

Anxiety is that indicator light. You may feel it in your stomach or throat, or in your chest where your heart races *as if you are in danger.*

> **That's your indicator.**
> **That's how you know**
>> **you are believing the doubt. The lies.**

And it hurts, **because it should.**

It feels like death, **because it should,**

> so you'll wake up, so you'll notice:

> *something needs my attention, something isn't right here.*

So don't be angry with anxiety. Anxiety is trying to tell you something. It's sounding an alarm so loud, so intense,

> so you will listen.

Here is what to do when you feel this.

Just pause.
> **Notice the intense emotion,**
>> **and let it bring your awareness to your body first.**

Locate the emotion in your body by asking questions.

Where do I feel this emotion specifically in my body?

> Is it in my stomach,
> shoulders,

chest,
or heart?

Then, describe how it feels.

Is it hot?
Cold?
Fast or slow?
Is it heavy?
Or fluttery?
Does it sting?
Does it move?

By asking these questions in your mind, you are like the mechanic seeing the red light, but you're not mad at it, avoiding it, or feeling shame that it's there.

You appreciate it for doing its job.

And you go to work to solve the problem.

You look here and there, you check the wires, **and you find it.**

Emotions just want to be found.

They want to be heard and understood.

And until they are, they get louder and more intense because they want to help you solve something quickly.

Once you know where this anxiety is in your body, and exactly how it feels for you,

find the thoughts creating it.

What were you believing?

> Notice the doubt, notice the lies.
> Hear them,
> and then question them.

Question them until you find the truth.

The truth about you never hurts.

When you believe what is true about you, it's warm, it's light, it gives you energy, it fills your cells with hope.

The truth about you always exists.

But when you doubt it, you stay stuck.

And when you believe it, you are free.

Chapter 21

THE LIES OTHERS HAVE TOLD US ABOUT OURSELVES

Throughout our lives, we've been told lies about who we are, what we can achieve, and what's possible for us. We're flooded with millions of others' opinions about our identities, and as I've mentioned before, most thoughts tend to be negative, so it can be extremely hard to believe we are worthy and capable as we hear more negativity than positivity about ourselves—both from others and from ourselves.

Thoughts are just thoughts; they are random, unfiltered, unquestioned, and rarely factual. They cannot make or break who you are. They do not hold any power over you,

unless

you believe them to be true.

Then they are an extremely powerful force in your life.

When thoughts are believed, they hold power over your emotions, choices, behavior, ability, and all of the results in your life.

When women drink in the condescending lies that are told to them throughout their lives—about who they are and who they are not, what they can and cannot be or do—and they believe those lies, a dark cloud of self-doubt forms over their heads. No one's words can create this cloud. They do not have the power to. This cloud is created when **you believe those words.** This dark cloud that covers you in fear, insecurity, uncertainty, and doubt is not permanent, and **you hold all the power to let it dissipate.**

All the power.

The words you have heard about who you are *are never facts.* Remember, the brain doesn't often think or speak in facts. The brain guesses, assumes, and imagines because it doesn't know ultimate truth—*your mind has only been alive as long as you have.* But your soul has lived much longer and **knows truth when you hear it.**

Whatever you have been told in your life, however painful, you are allowed to question it. And if it doesn't feel like truth to your soul, it's not yours to keep. Releasing it is a job you must do for yourself. No one else can do it for you. Take time to think about what you believe is true about you. Write those things down, and then read them out loud and notice how you feel when you think about them.

These are some of the most common ones I hear when I coach women.

- No one takes me seriously.
- I am not good enough.
- I'm overweight.
- I don't know what I'm doing.
- I'm not a good mom.
- I have no friends.
- No one likes me.
- Something is wrong with me.

- I'm not very smart.
- I'm a mess.
- I am too much.
- I don't fit in.

Have you ever thought any of these thoughts before? Or is this a shocking list to see? You, me, and everyone on the planet has believed some or all of the thoughts on this list at some point. Notice how these are not new thoughts. These thoughts have been circulating this world as long as humans have been here. Your negative thoughts about yourself aren't novel, and they are definitely not true. Millions of people are having the exact same thoughts about themselves as we speak.

Close your eyes, and ask yourself what the most common negative thoughts are that you have about yourself. Write them down here.

_____

_____

_____

_____

_____

_____

_____

_____

_____

_____

Now, read each one out loud to yourself, pausing after each one to notice how you feel in your body when you hear it. If you feel heavy, sad, defeated, anxious, hurt, lonely—anything that makes you sink or question your worth—**that thought *is a lie.***

How you feel when you think it **is how you know if it's true or not.**

It's a simple yet powerful tool we were all given by the Divine.

We need to drop into the body and feel to find truth because brains don't tell the truth.

Words don't have to be true for the brain to believe them.

Once you notice what is true and what isn't, you now have a way to guide yourself. You will begin to build trust with yourself to know what is true and what is false about yourself, never leaving it up to anyone else ever again.

It is always yours to decide.

Often, women accept breadcrumbs because they don't believe they are enough. Every tiny breadcrumb of a compliment feels like a breath of life. Women will do almost anything for it because they are starving themselves of any praise.

They don't allow themselves to notice their beauty, knowledge, capabilities, talents, gifts, or strengths, so it's incredibly hard to believe they are amazing, powerful, and worthy and have incomprehensible value. Instead, they spend their energy wishing they were as good as someone else.

This leaves them depleted and insecure *only because they are believing lies* about themselves rather than what is true.

EVERY thought that limits you is a lie!

Every. Single. One.

God doesn't limit you.

You limit you!

People can offer you their thoughts, opinions, and ideas about you, but YOU choose to either take those things in and believe them or disagree and not feel hurt by them.

All thoughts are OPTIONAL.

But all of them have power IF YOU LET THEM.

If you deplete yourself all day with thoughts of not being enough of anything for anyone,

then you will be starving for anyone's breadcrumbs.

And you will crave any attention, even if it hurts you in the end.

You will give up your body, your time, your possibilities, and your creations for

- cheap attention,
- a drop of dopamine,
- fake intimacy,
- a simple touch,
- cheesy compliments,
- mere words, or
- a combination of all of these.

You will give people what *they* want and need for a nibble of a nice word in return.

But not anymore.

Because you are remembering who you are, and with each page of this book that you turn, you will stand stronger, having more awareness of the divine being you are.

No more believing the lies that others have told you.

No more breadcrumbs.

You are a direct descendant of the Divine. Feel it and be it.

Chapter 22

THE LOOP OF PERFECTIONISM

We are often taught to believe that God is judging us, expecting us to demonstrate our love through perfection. This belief fuels a relentless cycle of striving for perfection as a means to earn love.

I used to try to be perfect for everyone because I totally linked it to being loved. Before anyone would come over, I would clean my house to make it look like nobody lived there, cleaning places no one would ever look. I'd change my clothes and fix my hair. I would make sure everything was in place, and I was perfectly ready.

If perfection were a requirement for love, then no one would be lovable. Without imperfections, there would be no room for choices, mistakes, mercy, or grace.

Mothers find joy in their children's imperfect creations, as does God.

As mothers, we feel joy that our children are learning and creating. Everything they create means something to us.

What if we believed God's love is like a mother's love,

how would we feel?

Would it feel more safe to try new things, even if it wasn't perfect?

Would we be more excited to show God what we have created?

Would we give ourselves more acceptance and grace?

Would we feel more wanted and loved as we are?

What would change for you if you thought your Heavenly Mother loved you like you loved your newborn child?

A newborn doesn't earn our love. They didn't *do* anything for us.

In my pregnancy, all I felt was pain, sickness, discomfort, and depression.

If we *add up the pain* . . . I should hate the baby when it's born. My baby didn't *do* anything *for* me. What did I gain, other than fifty pounds?

> It hurt.
> I got less done.
> I felt uncomfortable constantly.
> I was sick 24-7.

I should blame the baby for all of that pain when it's born. But when I hold my baby in my arms,

> I have no anger,
> I have no regret,
> I have no blame.

I only have love.

How is that possible?

Because a mother's love isn't earned or deserved. It isn't measured by our doings or what we accomplish. We don't have to prove we are anything to receive it.

It exists and we exist.

So as that child grows, they can bring any messy, imperfect creation to their mother, and she cheers!

When they draw shapes that don't exist or letters that don't look like letters,

> color outside of the lines,
> sing the wrong words to the song,
> count 1-2-3-6-9-10,
> talk with a lisp or pronounce everything wrong,

our mothers smile and soak it in. *They write it down and keep it.*

They don't need it to be correct or perfect to love their child. Mothers just want us as we are, as we learn—imperfect but perfectly lovable.

If we are not doing, working, proving, or earning we think no one will love us.

But that is a lie.

Love has nothing to do with our doings!

And we see that as we watch mothers love their children. Children do nothing—and I mean nothing—perfectly.

They aren't supposed to. And if they did, would it be so lovable?

Perfection is the thief of love, creativity, humanness, and connection.

Think of someone you love or admire, someone you just love being around.

Do you love them because they are flawless? Because . . .

> they got straight A's in high school;
>
> they always look perfect;
>
> they have a perfectly clean house;
>
> you weighed them, and they are just the right amount of pounds;
>
> they have never been late;
>
> they have never burned dinner;
>
> they have perfect children;
>
> they make the right amount of money;
>
> they have never doubted or been confused;
>
> they are never sad, scared or overwhelmed?

Do you love them because they are perfect? Or do you love how *you* feel around them?

Do you like yourself more around them?

Do you feel more comfortable?

Do you have more fun?

Are they relatable and make you feel like you're not alone in the messiness of life?

Do you see their mistakes and feel more comfortable about yours?

Perfection doesn't make us feel love for someone.

Imperfection does!

As women, we get sucked into a loop of perfection because we believe it is how we will be loved and accepted. We forget how we love our children unconditionally.

We can't see that we are loved that way, too, by God. Yes, God—both our Divine Mother and Father—who need no offerings of perfection,

> who see no flaws,
> take no measurements,
> who don't make lists or check them twice,
> do not add up your value at the end of the day
> and then only love you to the amount you've earned.

Our Gods delight in what you create, how you feel, and **who you are**, knowing that perfection in our minds has a vastly different meaning than it does in Theirs.

To God, perfect means you are complete. It never was a measurement of what you do or what you earn.

Create your life from the energy of love, not perfection, and you will shift the focus of your life to abundance instead of scarcity, which will change everything. When you see yourself as lovable in your messy moments—when you are late or forget to make dinner, when you think you are overweight, too old, not smart enough, not a good mom, not good at everything you want to be good at—you will find a peace inside yourself no one else can give you. You won't be anxious and depleted at the end of every day, filled with mom guilt, spinning in shame. You will feel centered and know that you are loved perfectly in and through all of those moments, just as you love your children in theirs. I know it's frustrating to live with messy, imperfect little humans. It's exhausting! And believe me, it is the hardest thing I've ever done, but how I love them is constant.

Deciding to change my belief about perfection and how God loves me has given me a peace I could never find before, a stillness inside myself and a freedom to stop measuring my day against someone else's. These new thoughts gave me confidence that I am enough as I am, and so is everyone else. It helped me to see myself as a lovable, messy, engaging, and adorable child of a Divine Mother, who I imagine watches me with a smile, laughing, nodding, cheering, and protecting me, as I do my own children.

I didn't change God; God is what God is. All I did was change how I imagined God, how I thought about God, and how I thought about myself. And it changed my whole inner world.

I let go of perfection because I could see it for the lie it was, how it keeps so many stuck in its painful loop of never doing or being enough, living in anxiety, worry, and doubt. I didn't want to live life that way anymore. Life is too precious and goes too fast.

These new thoughts, over time, helped me believe,

I no longer need to be perfect to feel safe, or loved.

And this is my hope for you as well, my friend.

Chapter 23

LOVE BEYOND THE RULES

Whenever we try to lead people to God out of fear, lack, or scarcity, we're acting out of a desire for control and ego, trying to make them believe the way we want them to. In doing so, we lose the essence of love and who God truly is.

In many religions, people often get so lost in the weeds of following rules for God's love, grace, and blessings that they miss the whole point and purpose of God. Our brains can get stuck believing it's the rules that make us worthy, lovable, and safe. We hyperfixate on these rules and, in the process, lose love, connection, influence, and impact. This has happened for centuries across all religions, not out of malicious intent but because of the scarcity of the mind and the power of the ego.

It can be challenging to allow people their agency, to trust that they can connect with God differently than we do and that God will protect and love them even when they aren't following our rules. I believe most religions started with the intent to connect with God and teach people the best way to live. We have a human desire for everyone's safety and well-being, so we seek God's help thinking it's the ultimate protection.

However, our brains bring our beliefs, ideas, rules, regulations, limits, and deep-seated fears into the picture. Just like the Pharisees in the Bible, who desired righteousness and wanted to please God, many of us let our brains create the rules for God. Left unmanaged, our brains often spin out of control, guessing and creating from fear. This spin led the Pharisees to establish numerous rules and restrictions: what you could and couldn't eat or drink, what you couldn't say or do, what you had to wear, how many steps you could take, and who you could speak with and when. They believed these rules were the way to God, blessings, hope, and safety for all.

The rules became their focus, and what the brain focuses on, it creates more and more of. Eventually, the Pharisees equated the rules with God. Rules then *became* their God, and they were committed to these rules above all I don't blame them; I can see their intentions and what their minds thought was best. This is human, but it is not God.

The Pharisees focused so much on rule-breaking, consequences, and those not adhering to the rules that they lost sight of love. When we focus on the *conditions* of love, we lose love. They lost sight of the love, safety, faith, and abundance they sought and instead fixated on lack, fear, worry, flaws, and conditions.

They wasted their energy counting steps instead of connecting with people. They looked for what people were lacking instead of how they could love them, learn from them, and help them. They spent hours and days in their churches, devising punishments for rule-breaking instead of seeking goodness, light, and hope for all. They failed to see people as inherently worthy and welcome.

So when Jesus came—the very One they were trying to serve and please—they couldn't recognize Him. They didn't believe in Him and couldn't love Him because He didn't follow their rules.

> He talked to all people,
> loved all people,
> healed all people,
> spent time with people,
> listened to them,
> walked with them,
> and fed them.

He did what the Pharisees wouldn't. He loved instead of condemned. He healed instead of abandoned.

And the Pharisees hated Him. The God they so longed to please through rule-keeping was standing right in front of them, performing miracles, yet they couldn't see Him because they were fixated on how *He* was breaking *their* conditions for love, acceptance, hope, and healing.

The rules became their God, and God became the rule in their minds.

Remember this the next time you find yourself obsessing over the rules you believe everyone needs to follow to be loved,

> **especially the rules you hold for yourself to be loved, accepted, and worthy.**

Section 6

POWER OF THOUGHTS, AGENCY, AND CHOICE

THE POWER OF YOUR THOUGHTS SHAPES YOUR REALITY AND GUIDES YOUR CHOICES. WHAT YOU CREATE FOR YOURSELF COMES FROM WHAT YOU BELIEVE YOU DESERVE.

Chapter 24

THE COACHING MODEL

I want to help you learn how to WORK WITH the brain. In this chapter, I will teach you the model I use as a coach that helps so many people change their lives. This model will empower you and help you know what you control and what you don't. If you put your focus on what you control, you will create your life with intention instead of waiting, wishing, and hoping for your life to turn out well.

The Model

We all experience these five things:

1. **Circumstances**
2. **Thoughts**
3. **Feelings**
4. **Actions**
5. **Results**

Circumstances are neutral. Yes, neutral, even though none of us think they are. These are the facts of life, things like the weather, age, height, weight, and anything that happens outside of you: anything someone says to you or about you, how many toys are left on the floor, how much money is in your bank account, what religion you belong to, others' words, or opinions people have, etc.

Circumstances are things we can agree exist, things we see, hear, or measure.

Thoughts are how your brain *interprets circumstances*. This is where your brain decides if they are good or bad, right or wrong, if you like them or don't.

Your thoughts create the *meaning* of circumstances.

Feelings are energy in motion in the body, vibrations that we can sense and feel. We've assigned various names to describe these sensations, such as

- happy,
- sad,
- anxious,
- worried,
- scared,
- angry,
- insecure,
- doubtful,
- afraid,
- grief,
- overwhelm, or
- disappointment.

Even though we have names to describe this energy and vibration in the body, these emotions may not feel the same for everyone. Sadness might feel heavy in one person's chest and queasy in someone else's stomach. Anxiety might feel like a fluttery heart and tingly hands to one person or nausea and dizziness to another.

This is important to know.

How we feel is the *fuel* for what we do—the action we take or don't take.

Think of a Ferrari. Most people think of this car as fast! This car was built to go fast, but if you filled up this Ferrari with the wrong fuel, it wouldn't go as fast or as far. It may not even go at all.

Is it because the Ferrari was made wrong, or is just not enough?

No!

It just needs the right fuel to do what it is made to do.

It's the same with all of us!

Emotion is the body's fuel for action. It's the reason and energy for what we do or don't do.

Emotion is the brain's only reward. The reason we do anything is for how we *think* it will *feel*.

Nothing matters more to the brain than avoiding pain and seeking pleasure, so it is highly motivated by emotion.

Think of a time when you felt really sad or depressed. What did your actions look like, and how did you do them? Were you pushing through a workout, coming up with new ideas, or organizing your drawers? Were you painting, or dancing to music? Or were you avoiding tasks and people, moving more slowly, and just waiting for the day to end?

You are still the Ferrari, but when you feel discouraged, doubtful, or sad, the car moves slower. And that is OK! Nothing is wrong with the

Ferrari when it has the wrong fuel. *And nothing is wrong with you when you feel an emotion you don't like.*

Just notice it.

And let it make sense instead of judging the car because it has the wrong fuel. The car wasn't made wrong and its value is exactly the same; it just runs differently with different fuel.

And so do you!

For contrast, think about what actions you take when you feel

- motivated,
- excited,
- hopeful.

How do you act? What do you do? Do you choose to do different things? Do you do more or less? And how are you doing it?

When I experience these emotions, I show up very differently. I am more fun, connected, and engaged. I plan things with friends, check in on other people, and come up with new ideas for my future.

It's not because I'm a better person that day. It's not because the circumstances changed. I'm still me with the same house and the same children. I have the same value when I feel sadness or disappointment. But when I generate more powerful emotions, I act differently, move differently, speak differently, and create differently.

I'm still a Ferrari no matter how I feel, **and so are you**—just as valuable and capable.

Your feelings don't MEAN anything about who you are and what you're capable of. They are just information for you. They are *for you*.

They help you be able to tune in to your body and slow down or speed up if needed.

Emotions don't make you good or bad, right or wrong.

You will just take different actions based on how you feel at any given moment.

Here is a summary of the model I just explained

Circumstances: neutral until we have a thought about them

Thoughts: our interpretation and meaning of circumstances

Feelings: vibrations in the body

Actions: what we do or don't do based on how we feel

Results: what we have created for ourselves from our thoughts, feelings, and actions

The only thing you don't have control over all of the time is the **circumstance**.

The rest is yours.

We all have circumstances, and the reason we don't *feel* the same way about them is *how we think* about them. **The meaning we assign to circumstances creates how we feel about them.**

This is why we don't *feel* the same way about

- politics,
- religion,
- God,

- weather,
- relationships, or
- money . . .

because our thoughts create our emotions.

We don't need to be confused about why others don't do what we do or feel the same way about certain things.

It's simple.

They just think and feel differently about it than you do!

One circumstance we have many different thoughts, beliefs, and feelings about is God.

Let's use God as a circumstance and look at it in the model we just learned:

*Let's say **this** is your friend's model.*

Circumstance: God

Thought: "God doesn't love me."

Feeling: Hopeless

Action (possible actions taken from this thought and feeling):

- Don't pray with intention, believing it will be answered.
- Don't think about God often.
- Act as if you are on your own, and try to do everything yourself.

- Fixate on survival.
- Doubt miracles.
- Resent or distrust people who love God or promote religion.
- Avoid prayer, religious meetings, gatherings, or music.

Result: You don't allow yourself to feel loved by God.

*Let's say **this** is your friend's model.*

Circumstance: God (same as yours)

Thought: "God is love."

Feeling: Peace

Action (possible actions taken from this thought and emotion):

- Pray, believing you will receive.
- Ask for help and guidance.
- Trust you will be given what you need.
- Listen to music that speaks of a loving God.
- Join groups or gatherings that teach of a loving God.
- Speak of God.
- Pray for others and yourself.
- Act as if you are loved.
- Expect miracles beyond what you can do for yourself.

Result: YOU are loving, and believe you are loved by God.

It's very important to note that neither of these models is right or wrong, I'm just giving examples from clients I have worked with in the past to show you actions one might take based on what they are thinking and how they are feeling. Again, neither of these models is the "right" one. They are just different. But both make sense, and *both are allowed.*

You and your friend are just creating different experiences and results **for yourselves**.

You and your friend have the same circumstance—God—and that is neutral until you have thoughts and create meanings about God.

You both just **think** about it differently, which generates different **emotions** that fuel you to take different **actions** which create different **results**.

It can be easy to judge people **for how they feel and what they do.** But if you understood how they thought about it, it would all make sense.

If you believed and felt exactly as they did, you would do the same things they do.

I have witnessed hundreds of clients experience "light bulb" moments of clarity as we work through their challenges with this tool. They initially believe they need to change their external circumstances to feel better, only to realize that the key to feeling better is adjusting their thoughts about their circumstances. By choosing a thought that resonates more truthfully and inspires action rather than inaction, they find relief in minutes.

While some circumstances like where you live, your marital status, or your job, can be changed, many are beyond your control—such as your age, height, the weather, your children's personalities and choices, your spouse's weaknesses or choice of words, what your friends say about you, who likes you, the current president, your neighbors' actions, or the rules and beliefs of your religion.

Relentlessly focusing on changing circumstances beyond your control can lead to frustration and a sense of hopelessness. **When we put our energy toward what we are powerless over, we suffer.**

We don't have control over other people, their words, feelings, or actions. But we always have control over ourselves.

Let this empower you!

If you put your focus on the parts of the model you control—

thoughts,

feelings,

actions,

and results—

you will create a powerful, intentional life! You will know that you can adjust your thinking whenever you feel afraid, stuck, stressed, anxious, angry, or hopeless, and quickly transform those emotions into feelings that will create the results you actually want.

If you often feel like a victim to your circumstances, know that you can change the way you're thinking about it. Choose what you want to make it mean about you, choose what you want to believe, choose a thought that feels true but propels you forward instead of keeping you stuck in the past.

Here are two models I have experienced in my own life. The first one is my "Unintentional Model," where I reacted to the circumstance without intention. The other is an example of how I **chose** to reinterpret the circumstance to create a different result for myself.

Unintentional model:

Circumstance: My kid said "I hate you mom. You are doing it all wrong."

Thought: He is so mean and ungrateful.

Feeling: Anger

Action: Shut down and give him the silent treatment—don't respond—then lose my temper—react from anger—become more aggressive and talk about how *he* is doing it wrong, put him in his room, close the door, and cry.

Result: I am mean and ungrateful at that moment.

Notice how my thought ends up being the result I create for myself. **When I think he is mean and ungrateful, I become mean and ungrateful.** Our thoughts always lead to the results; they are the map telling the body what to create.

Intentional model: this is the model I created with intention for all those times when my kids say things I don't want to hear.

Circumstance: My kid said "I hate you mom. You are doing it all wrong" (or any other statement they say when upset).

Thought: Sometimes I do it wrong, and that's OK. I know I am a good mom.

Feeling: Centered

Action: Be more patient—ask him questions about why he is frustrated—and apologize for my part; let him know he is allowed to be angry but not disrespectful—talk it through with him—and give him a consequence that feels right and within reason.

Result: I'm the mom I want to be.

When I changed the thought or the meaning about what my child said, it changed the rest of my model **automatically**. That thought generated a whole different emotion, which allowed me to stay centered and react in a way that felt more true to the mom I want to be.

Your thoughts are always leading the way, guiding you to results. They are a powerful frequency and a tool for creating your life. Even when you don't notice, even when others seem to make things hard, and even when you wish for different results, you are the creator of your experience. If you want change, start by shifting how you think about the circumstance, the problem, or the person. You'll see how this alters how you feel and what you do automatically.

I've run thousands of models and watched as clients have tackled their toughest challenges. I've seen women transform how they communicate with their spouses, moms change how they react to their most difficult child, strained relationships become safe and connected, and people finally lose the weight they felt stuck with. Women shift from victims to leaders in their homes. Clients' businesses transform and thrive. It all continues to amaze me, the sheer power of our thoughts. God has given us so much power, control, and choice to create our lives. Changing one simple word in a thought can have a huge impact.

A simple way to release shame is to add "AND THAT'S OK" to the end of your thought.

"I don't like when my husband is upset, and that's OK."

"I am disappointed with my friend, and that's OK."

"I messed up today and I'm really upset with myself, and that's OK."

"Of course my kids are frustrated. I am too sometimes, and that's OK."

Saying "that's OK" isn't about settling but recognizing you're human. It's OK not to like everything or to get frustrated, and it's OK to make mistakes. This simple phrase helps lift that heaviness so you feel more movable, curious, and ready to find solutions.

Or you can add:

AND I'M FIGURING IT OUT, or

AND I'M LEARNING, or

AND I KNOW WHAT I NEED TO DO.

For example:

"I don't exercise like I want to, AND I'm figuring it out a little every day."

"I feel stuck in my marriage, AND I know what I need to do."

"I'm sick of feeling resentful in my marriage, AND I'm learning how to communicate my needs better."

Adding "and" at the end of your thought and reminding yourself that you are figuring it out, learning, and knowing what to do can change the meaning and intensity of the painful thought that kept you stuck.

The model is a tool I use daily with clients, and myself to create my life in the way I want instead of leaving it up to circumstance or needing others to change.

Thoughts are optional. We get to choose them. And by choosing them, we can generate emotion on purpose. Wait, what? Yes! *This means we have way more power and control over how we feel and what we create than anyone ever taught us.*

And if we can generate our emotions, we get to *choose* what fuel we give ourselves, which impacts how we act.

And this, my friend, is how you create your results on purpose. Yes, **create them.**

You are a creator, as is God.

God created by thought, *and so do you.*

If you want a certain result, you now know how to get there much faster than hoping and wishing. You can use this model to create it. Think of what you want, and work backward in the model to see what you would need to think, feel, and do to create it.

This is the power you always have. You can take this anywhere, and get in the driver's seat of your life. No more riding in the backseat holding on for dear life, hoping someone else takes you where you want to go and makes you feel what you want to feel.

Chapter 25

CREATE YOUR LIFE WITH
THE POWER OF THOUGHT

Thoughts tell the brain what evidence to look for, and then the brain goes to work looking for how its thoughts are true. Your brain has thousands of thoughts a day, and most are not factual or true. They are random optional ideas, guesses, and assumptions. Thoughts send signals to your body and generate each emotion. This is one reason thoughts are so powerful: they create energy in the body, and from that energy we take action. We make choices, we engage or disengage. We create or we stay stuck because of these different emotional signals.

When we aren't aware of what we are thinking and the emotion our thought is generating, we lose power and control over what we do and what we create.

Imagine you're setting off on a long drive and I ask you to count the red and white cars you see along the way, and then report back. When you return, you tell me you spotted ten red cars and twenty-two white ones. However, if I then ask how many black cars you saw, you might not recall seeing any. Even if there were more black cars than red ones on the road, you might believe there were none simply because your brain wasn't focused on noticing them.

It's easy to be convinced there were no black cars because you weren't primed to look for them.

We see what we are looking for. And if I primed your brain by telling it what evidence to look for, it would only focus on those two colors and toss out every other color as irrelevant.

This can become a problem when we apply this pattern to ourselves or others. Our thoughts condition our brains to seek out certain realities, much like scanning for a specific car color. If you frequently think, "No one likes me," your brain will actively search for evidence to support that belief, noticing only what confirms it and ignoring anything that contradicts it.

For example, if you believe a particular person in your life doesn't love you, you'll constantly search for evidence to confirm this belief. You'll focus on the times they don't call rather than when they do. Any attention they give will never be the right amount. You will fixate on their mistakes and flaws more than what they do right. You'll scrutinize their tone and facial expressions, perceiving them as insincere. Even if they hug you, you might interpret it as an act of obligation rather than genuine affection. Every action they take will serve as *proof* of their lack of love because you've conditioned your brain to view it that way.

You will believe they don't love you because you are not looking for any evidence that they do (just like not noticing any black cars because you weren't looking for them).

And over time this one random, simple thought your brain offered you will become a belief. It will seem so true, so factual that you will believe it no matter how much evidence you've actually seen to the contrary. It's just like if you only looked for red and white cars, you would start to believe that those are the only colors of cars and the other colors don't exist.

Evidence that doesn't fit our thoughts or beliefs gets tossed out.

The brain doesn't want to spend energy on what it doesn't believe. So even when someone compliments you, invites you, or offers to help you, your brain won't register it as them liking you. It will come up with some other reason they are there; you will wonder if it's out of obligation or pity. But you won't allow yourself to believe it's because they simply like you, want to help or be your friend.

I have seen this so many times in my life: women who don't believe they are enough for anyone, *especially God.*

They give me all the evidence of this belief, pulling up memories from when they were eight, twelve, fifteen, and twenty years old— describing moments when they didn't feel good enough, comments people made at school, breakups or divorces, loss of friends, low income, a messy house, their weight or pant size, how they don't get enough done, that they are disorganized. The list goes on and on, all evidence the brain has gathered for years and years **to prove the thought "true" that they aren't good enough.**

Have you ever met someone who really lives into this type of belief? She constantly talks about her flaws, shortcomings, shape, and size as if none of it is ever quite right. She talks about all the things she wishes she could change about herself to be better,

    to finally be enough.

And if you compliment her she gets defensive and even angry at times. If you offer her evidence that she is loved, beautiful, worthy, or brilliant, she will disagree. She may even laugh and say, "You're crazy! You don't know what you're talking about."

And maybe, this is you.

Maybe you have believed this thought, and many others along the way, fighting for your "not enoughness," rejecting compliments *while desperately needing them at the same time.*

Whatever you believe about yourself **will always feel the most true.**

Just like there are not *only* red and white cars on the road, we are not *only* flawed or lacking. We are also a million other things we don't notice about ourselves. We are more than our brain can comprehend. The good about us is far greater than what is lacking.

But if we constantly believe our limiting thoughts, those thoughts are all we will see.

I'm talking to you!

What you think about you will look for.

What you look for you will find.

What you find will seem true.

Our beliefs are the walls we live within. We have built these walls ourselves, and they eventually feel like a prison that keeps us stuck, quiet, unsure, and anxious.

What mental walls have you built around yourself with your thoughts and beliefs about who you are? Over time, you've added layers to these walls with more evidence, making them taller and stronger until they start to suffocate you, filling you with anxiety, fear, and self-doubt. It's hard to breathe, dream, or express yourself freely within these walls. They keep you feeling small, isolated, and fearful of being truly seen. You hide behind them, hoping no one notices your perceived flaws, *thinking you're doing the world a favor by shrinking down and disappearing into the darkness.*

You didn't build these walls intentionally, so there is no need to judge yourself for them. *Simply notice them.* Notice them as the lies that they are—lie after lie you once thought and then believed to build these walls brick by brick. Notice how it feels to live within these heavy walls, wishing someone would save you. But if they try, you beat them off because you *believe this prison is your truth.* This cage has become your home, and somehow it feels more comfortable than the actual truth. **So you stay,** not because anyone put you there, for they cannot.

It's not because God created you imperfectly, not because you deserve less.

It's only because you believed the lies your brain made up about you.

If you can believe lies, then you can also believe the truth. And at first, the truth will *feel like the lie.* It will contradict a lifetime of evidence that you are unlovable, the wrong size, too much or too little of what is good, and never enough.

I believe that limits are lies.

Any thoughts or belief that limits you—who you are, what you are capable of—is a lie. God will never limit you. God doesn't work in limits. God works in vast abundance, and you are vastly abundant!

Think of God's creations—the sun, mountains, oceans, animals, space, air—are they not enough? Are the mountains not tall enough, the oceans not deep enough, or space not big enough?

No.

They are all more than enough, and so are you!

The same Heavenly Beings that made the universe, space, and time *made you*. And just like all of those things, you are more than your looks, more than your size, more than what you see, think, or believe—as all of God's creations are. We can't measure them all, we cannot comprehend them fully. And the same goes for you.

Stop measuring your enoughness; it is immeasurable. It is far too vast for your human mind to comprehend.

Put that thought down, and walk away.

Take a few minutes to close your eyes and imagine who you would be if you really believed you were more than enough for anyone, for anything you wanted, and for yourself. Imagine that you didn't question your worth. You just knew it was 100%, not imagining you are conceited or believing you're better than others but just completely worthy, capable, and lovable. You have everything inside you to be happy, to have success, to be who you want to be in your relationships.

Imagine this in every detail you can. And write your answers here or somewhere you will see often.

How would you communicate with those you love if you believed you were enough for them?

_____

_____

_____

_____

_____

_____

_____

_____

_____

What would you say yes to?

_____

_____

_____

_____

_____

_____

_____

_____

_____

What would you say no to?

_____

_____

_____

_____

_____

_____

_____

_____

_____

What choices would you make if you didn't lack confidence, security, or love for yourself?

_____

_____

_____

_____

_____

_____

_____

_____

_____

What would you eat if you deeply appreciated your body and were grateful for how it gives you life everyday?

_____

_____

_____

_____

_____

_____

_____

_____

What would you talk about if you allowed your voice and passion to be heard and believed it would have an impact?

_____

_____

_____

_____

_____

_____

_____

_____

What are you accepting now that would you no longer accept if you didn't fear rejection?

_____

_____

_____

_____

_____

_____

_____

_____

_____

How would you feel if you genuinely liked yourself?

_____

_____

_____

_____

_____

_____

_____

_____

What would you do or stop doing?

_____

_____

_____

_____

_____

_____

_____

How would you show up in your relationships?

_____

_____

_____

_____

_____

_____

_____

_____

How would liking yourself impact your decisions?

_____

_____

_____

_____

_____

_____

_____

_____

_____

Notice all that would change by changing this one thought and belief alone.

This is the power God gave you in your mind and your body. When you believe thoughts that are **true** about you,

> you generate useful, powerful emotions, you take new action, and you create the results you desire.

Don't leave this job to anyone else. It's not their responsibility to create your life experience.

It is yours.

What a gift!

Chapter 26

MOVIES OF THE MIND

Your brain and body are more brilliant and more capable than you are aware of. They are constantly working to keep you alive so that your soul can have the experience it was meant to have here on earth.

If you listen to and believe every thought your brain offers you, you will often feel fearful. And you will believe there is danger everywhere.

Your brain scans for danger because it wants to be prepared for it, so it runs ahead of the present moment and imagines what could go wrong. It will imagine all kinds of scenarios trying to prepare you for all kinds of dangerous possibilities.

The brain generally doesn't conjure up delightful, fun, or easy scenarios, nor does it focus on what could go right, because it knows there's no need to prepare for those. It doesn't have to solve the easy and enjoyable aspects of life for survival.

Instead, your mind fixates on worst-case scenarios, letting them unfold like movies in your mind that stir up worry, anxiety, and fear—much like a scary movie at home can make you feel tense and frightened. Your body reacts to what you envision just as it does to what you watch. When you mentally play out these dire scenarios, it feels as though they're happening in real time, similar to watching a movie filled with danger, pain, or horror can make those events seem real to you and generate distress in the body.

It's crucial to understand that your brain cannot distinguish between actual events and what you vividly imagine.

When you first turn on a movie, you know it's not real, but the longer you watch the more your body feels as if you are *in* the movie. You may feel nervous, anxious, or afraid, and as the movie continues to play you start to sweat. You curl your feet up onto the couch and pull a blanket over you. You try to solve for the danger as if you're in it, and you start to believe you need to save yourself.

Your body reacts to whatever it's observing, whether it's a movie on a screen or a scenario you're imagining about work, a social event, a decision, or a difficult conversation. The way you envision these situations will generate your emotional experience and influence how you approach the situations, and you'll behave as though your imagination is the reality—similar to how we start to believe movies are real.

But when you turn the movie off, look around the room, and realize no one is chasing you, nothing bad is happening, and you are safe, your heart rate begins to slow down, you come to the present, and you let out a sigh of relief because you realize what is actually real.

Have you ever wondered why your body experiences such a wide range of emotions over just two hours? Before starting the movie, you felt calm, relaxed, maybe even bored. But as it played, your body shifted into fight-or-flight mode as it experienced panic or fear. Once the movie ended, you returned to a state of calm and went to bed.

Throughout it all, your circumstances didn't change; you remained on the same couch in the same room. Yet, the thoughts and images running through your mind caused you to feel an intense spectrum of emotions.

The same thing happens when we live into the movies in our minds: our made-up worst-case scenarios. Before we go anywhere, we think about all the ways we will be embarrassed, or we will mess up, people will laugh, we will do something stupid, and no one will like us. Your brain can create the most epic movie ahead of time, with all the intricate details—watching yourself fail, watching people laugh, and then feeling all the emotions you would feel in that moment—even if you're just sitting on the couch, safe as can be.

What you imagine, you feel.

Movies are designed to make us imagine and feel. The best actors are the ones that can generate the most emotion to make us believe and feel as if we are there.

The more you watch the reruns of these worst-case scenario movies in your mind, the more anxious you will feel.

Anxiety comes from believing made-up stories of a dangerous future.

The brain doesn't think it is relevant to play out best-case scenarios because it doesn't need to protect you from them.

> *Feeling anxious doesn't mean there is anything wrong with you.*

Your brain wants to help you. You just need to teach it what helps you and what doesn't.

Brains can be trained.

This is what I teach my clients who struggle with anxiety: that anxiety lives in the future, not the present.

I teach my clients to pause, or "turn off the movie in their mind," and notice that it's only a made-up story, just like you do when you turn off a scary movie at home and come back to the present moment. Ask yourself what you know to be true at that moment. Notice you are safe and have everything you need. Whatever story your brain projected into the future isn't what is happening right now.

A quick way to turn off the movie in your mind is to first notice how your body feels emotionally.

1. **Ask yourself, "How do I feel right now?"**

    Scared?
    Anxious?
    Worried?
    Doubtful?

2. Then ask yourself, "What movie am I watching in my mind right now?"

    Asking this question brings your brain's awareness to the story that is playing in your mind,

    so it can see it **without believing it**.

    This is so powerful! This is how you can notice it as a story instead of believing you are witnessing a true future.

3. Next, **tell yourself the truth**:

    This is why I feel the way I do, because I believe this story is real.

211

4. **Come to the present moment.**

What can you taste, touch, smell, see, or hear?

Use your five senses to bring you back to the present.

The present is where you are safe. *You can solve things in the present moment because you have all the puzzle pieces to* **decide and adjust.**

This will feel much more safe to the brain and the body.

When you train your brain to live more in the present and NOT in a scary movie about the future . . . your emotional life will change.

Just like your thoughts and imaginations can generate fear, they can also generate

- hope,
- motivation,
- peace,
- confidence,
- and miracles.

Imagining the future in a positive way is so powerful!

This is how we utilize the power of our minds and imaginations in a way that serves us and helps us create our lives intentionally.

As a coach, this is my magic.

I have helped many clients, particularly athletes, visualize their desired outcomes for future events. Rather than simply hoping their race or game turns out well, I guide them to envision it unfolding exactly as they wish, imagining how they want to perform. I have them close their eyes and describe each moment in vivid detail, and describe how they will feel when things go as planned. As they articulate these emotions, they experience those feelings right then and there by thought alone.

When we've linked their performance to a detailed emotional experience, it registers as a memory in the mind. The brain believes it has already happened that way. So, when they step into the game, their brain perceives their desired outcome as something already achieved, making it feel familiar and easier to execute.

For example, I was coaching a high school cross-country runner who was feeling frustrated and stuck. He wasn't improving in his races, he was falling behind and not reaching the times he wanted, so his mom sent him to me for help.

He had a major race coming up, the district meet just before the state competition. Having never qualified for state before, he was anxious to achieve it this year. If he could hit his target placement in this race, he would qualify for state for the first time.

As we met together I gathered information about his brain, most importantly how he thought about running and about himself—what he liked about racing, where he doubted, and when he felt confident. The brain is kind of like a science experiment to me. I gather the data and then I reorganize it so it can produce the desired outcome.

I asked him to describe the cross-country course that he would be running in the district meet—detailing the turns, hills, trees, etc. Then I had him close his eyes and imagine the exact thoughts he wanted to have, and how he wanted to feel as he warmed up for the race. And then again when he was on the starting line, I had him describe the emotion he wanted to generate to start the race. I had him explain his strategy for the first mile, then the second mile. We planned what he would think, feel, and do at each half-mile marker. We planned what he would do if someone passed him at a certain part of the course. He planned for each curve and hill. Then I had him decide where he *wanted* to feel a runner's high—the feeling that overcomes you with energy, power, and endurance making you feel like you can run forever. He told me exactly which curve, under which trees he wanted his runner's high to hit, and said that if it did he would be able to kick into another gear, pass people, and finish strong.

He then described epic music from his favorite movie playing in his mind as he pushed through the last 400 meters. And lastly, I had him describe how it would feel to finish at the exact placement he wanted to finish, knowing he had qualified for state for the first time. He described the euphoric feeling in great detail, and how he would hug his teammates and parents, and feel so proud of himself!

As he sat in the chair during our session, he vividly described each segment of the race, generating each emotion he desired in his race, and when he got to the part about experiencing a runner's high on the last curve, he opened his eyes and exclaimed, "Whoa, this is crazy! I feel a runner's high right now, and I'm not even running! I didn't know that was possible!" At that moment, he realized the incredible power of his mind, understanding how his thoughts generate emotions and how he could feel such a high purely through imagination.

I had him visualize the race in this exact way, with these exact emotions, many times before the day of his race. **And when the day came, he ran it exactly like he had imagined.** He passed people when he had planned on passing them, he felt all the emotions right when he had expected, the runner's high hit at the last curve, and the epic music filled his mind as he raced toward the finish line.

214

I'll never forget him recalling how incredible it felt to create his race ahead of time and then run it exactly like he had imagined. **He qualified for state for the first time** and was ecstatic! And so was I because I knew that he had learned how powerful he was in creating whatever result he wanted in his life—knowing that by choosing his thoughts, imagining how he wanted it to go, and then taking the action, he can make the impossible possible.

He is no longer anxious before his races, he knows exactly what to do and when, he trusts himself to execute, and knows he can generate the confidence he needs to reach his goals.

I've repeatedly witnessed this transformation in athletes I coach across various sports nationwide. I've helped them achieve remarkable results in sports I've never played myself. One of my clients, a high school football kicker, came to me as a junior. He was terrified of being the sole kicker on the team and anxious about making mistakes. He struggled to kick consistently and would often spiral into stress on the sidelines after missing a field goal, worried he'd miss the next one—which he often did—until we started working together.

Now he's a senior, his team is undefeated, and he's missed only one field goal all season! As a team captain, he leads his teammates in mindset strategies, helping them stay mentally focused even when trailing. He dedicates time alone before each game to get into a powerful mindset, and when practicing kicks into the net on the sidelines, he knows precisely what to focus on to remain confident and centered. He no longer allows negative energy to affect him, nor does he dwell on mistakes or missed kicks. Instead, he looks forward with certainty, and every time he steps onto the field, he trusts himself deeply—regardless of his coach's shouts from the sidelines or the points on the scoreboard—and he delivers! He no longer punts out of bounds or struggles with powerful kicks. I've watched him evolve from anxious, nervous, and doubtful to excited, confident, and centered! He has become a leader on and off the field because he now focuses on what he can control, and knows how to achieve his goals with ease.

Scan the code below for access to my course for athletes! This program is crafted to shift athletes from doubt, anxiety, and overthinking to renewed confidence, excitement, and motivation. Drawing from years of experience and proven tools and tips, this course will help athletes transform their performance and resilience so they can finally achieve their goals!

The movies you let play in your mind are powerful. They shape your emotions, influence your actions, and ultimately impact the outcomes you create for yourself. Don't let fear-filled stories keep playing, suggesting everything will go wrong, that you'll fail, or that no one will like you. That movie is old and boring by now! Take it out and replace it with the story of, "What if I succeed, what if it all works out, and what if it's better than I can even imagine?" Picture yourself succeeding, feeling confident, and getting what you want out of life. **This is the surest way to receive it!**

If you do this, you will no longer be a victim to the movies in your mind. Instead, you will become the director and YOU will be free to create the movie exactly how you want it to go.

Chapter 27

ALL-OR-NOTHING THINKING

No one can hand you a feeling. We often think we walk around giving people emotions, but we don't. We can impact and influence how people feel, making it easier for them to think certain kinds of thoughts. But we cannot force or give feelings.

This knowledge allows me to know that I can go anywhere and be my own safety because *I can generate the emotion I want instead of leaving that up to anyone else.*

I don't walk around soaking in others' thoughts and emotions like a sponge anymore, hoping for feelings, and then being disappointed that people didn't give them to me.

They can't.

Let this free you!

Let it free you from trying to control how everyone around you feels, free you from hoping, wishing, and waiting to feel how you want.

This is *agency*. Even God doesn't make us think certain thoughts or feel certain feelings. Everything is allowed so we can know for ourselves what is right for us and what we want.

It can be hard for our brains to allow things to be different from how we see them. Brains like to group things together into categories to make sense of them, often thinking in all-or-nothing terms.

- right/wrong
- good/bad
- happy/sad
- righteous/unrighteous
- hopeful/hopeless
- worthy/worthless

We think everything and everyone is either/or, all good or all bad.

But as humans we are both.

No one is all-or-nothing,

all good all the time or all bad all the time.

We aren't always happy or always sad.

We aren't all right or all wrong.

We live in the sometimes.

Sometimes we have hope, and sometimes we don't. And that doesn't make us right or wrong, good or bad. It makes us human, and *that is what we are supposed to be.* We are supposed to live in the sometimes. And there is *so* much more peace in allowing that.

Whenever we see ourselves or anyone else in an *all-or-nothing* way, we will feel pain **because it isn't true.**

Truth doesn't cause us to spin in anger, resentment, disappointment, or judgment. **Truth helps us move forward, find solutions, and take inspired action.**

The brain creates categories to sort information. These categories are usually very extreme because it takes more energy for the brain to find the center of all-or-nothing.

Imagine a continuum with "good" positioned at one extreme and "bad" at the opposite. Similarly, "right" sits at one end, while "wrong" is on the other. Between these ends, there are numerous possibilities gradually merging toward the center, offering a range of options along the way.

If we think that going to church is right and fits the "Good and Right" category, then we think every single person should go to church, no matter what, if they want to be good and right.

The way we think about things is what makes them feel right or wrong to us.

This is why we don't all agree on what is right and wrong. We simply have different thoughts about it. We don't agree on politics, religion, what is healthy, the best weather or place to live, or how much money someone should or shouldn't make. There's almost nothing that everyone agrees on because we all have different filters, experiences, and categories that our brains use to sort information into good or bad boxes.

No one can really fit into these made up all-or-nothing categories.

But it's easier for the brain to sort people that way so we can quickly decide if they are safe, trustworthy, or likable.

I've noticed this many times in my life. Watching as people meet someone new, one of the first things they will want to know is what religion they belong to, who they voted for, what they like, and what they believe in. They will ask this in creative ways, but all of it is the brain wanting to know if they are in the "Good and Right" category.

This is how the brain starts to gather the information it thinks is most relevant. We think, *if someone is of my religion, they must be safe to be around.* The brain then starts to assume and fill in the blanks about this new person it just met.

The brain doesn't need very many facts to assume it knows everything about someone.

For example, let's say you meet someone new and your brain asks the patterned questions to see if you should like them and if they are safe to be around. You find out they believe in your same religion, and their kids go to your kids' school. You learn they like yoga, and they love summer.

Your brain then goes to work filling in the blanks with what you know and what you have experienced as a measurement to see if the person is good or bad.

If they go to the same church you do, then you assume they believe it the same way you do. You then conclude they imagine God the same. Then they must be safe. The brain loves to assume it knows *without actually knowing.* It's easier and saves time without us having to ask someone about what they think or how they feel. We would rather just assume we know all about them when we have very little information.

221

The brain draws conclusions quickly, and it looks something like this:

If they go to church	**then they love Jesus.**
If they love Jesus	**then they are kind.**
If they are kind	**then they tell the truth.**
If they tell the truth	**then you can trust them.**
If you can trust them	**then they won't disappoint you.**
If they don't disappoint you	**then they are perfect.**
If they are perfect	**then they can do no wrong.**

And this is why you can get so excited about someone so quickly. The person only needs to give you four facts about themselves, and if you like those four facts, *you assume you'll like the rest.* But this sets you up for a lot of disappointment and confusion as you spend more time with this person. Over time, you will learn things about them that maybe you don't like or agree with, and your brain will be like, *wait, what? I thought you were only in the "Good and Right" category. You can't **not** invite me to a party if you are a member of my church because that's not what Jesus does, and you love Jesus, remember?*

How do we ever measure a person's rightness or wrongness, goodness or badness, enoughness or not enoughness? Our brains are always trying to measure it with our own filters that consist of what we believe. But **no one believes the same things, so we all measure with different rules.**

The truth is, there is no measuring tool to measure a human's value or worth.

I know that sounds obvious when you read it, but notice how often we are measuring each other with our own ideas—accepting, rejecting, and judging people based on little information and a lot of assumptions.

Some of us even believe we are doing the work of God when we do this, like, "Don't worry, God, I'll figure this out for you. Me and my brain will figure out who goes to Heaven and who doesn't. I got this! And then when I get up there I'll pull out my notebook and I'll let you know who gets in. I believe my thoughts are true, and so whoever I think is good, *is!*

You can trust me!"

We don't say it out loud, but our brains love thinking we are doing an important job, as if God can't quite see it or figure it out without our help.

Let me tell you this . . .

God doesn't see or put people in these boxes. God doesn't use human brain patterns, beliefs, agendas, or rules to judge, sort, or shift Their children.

That is what humans do. **But not God.**

God did not make us wrong, flawed, or not enough. And as much as we run around trying to figure out who God loves most or who is doing it right, we can never know *because we have human brains*: brains that assume the worst before the best; brains that judge and criticize without context; brains that think in worst-case scenarios; brains that live in scarcity, doubting more than we believe.

God doesn't do this.

God doesn't work in scarcity or not enoughness.

And God doesn't use fear or scarcity to try to force people into doing anything.

As I'm hoping you know by now, God is not singular. God is not man alone. And God doesn't use the limitations of a human mind that can only see what one mind has experienced as right or wrong.

God is plural—Man and Woman—two beings working in balance and harmony together. Not one above or better than the other but different, just like men and women here are different: different gifts, different ways of organizing, different things they bring to their children.

Men were never meant to rule over women. Men were never given more knowledge, strength, power, or purpose than women.

God the Father does not favor himself over our Mother. And together, They don't favor one of us over the other.

Our brains love to see differences as better than or less than because we are human. We have brains that measure worth with our *limited beliefs*. So of course, in our minds, no one is enough in some way or another.

The brain also doesn't think it needs to focus on abundance because it doesn't think it needs to solve for it. **So the brain focuses on the lack**—the lack in others and the lack in ourselves—**because it thinks it needs to solve for or fix or that.**

When all we see is the lack in others, we focus our time and energy on what we need to fix in people, *especially those we love most*.

And then we try to control, force, or manipulate people to be what we want them to be, and we miss all that they *are*. **We miss the magic, we miss the goodness, we miss their brilliance and what they are creating.**

If you notice yourself constantly worried about what is wrong with your children, your spouse, and yourself you will become anxious and angry because thoughts of lack generate feelings of anxiousness. **This is your sign to change your focus.**

Focus on the truth in people, not made-up ideas of who you *think* they should be. Try looking for the things in them that you don't need to solve for—the things that are already amazing, the things they are good at and what comes easily to them. **Notice how they are different from you but with intrigue, not critique.**

This will calm your fears and loosen your grip on trying to control everyone. And it will give you WAY more influence with those you love

     because

when people feel loved for who they already are, they feel safe to learn from you.

However, when you continually point out their mistakes, you lose influence as they begin to see you as a threat. They might try to appease you out of fear, but they won't respect you as someone to look up to and admire.

Loving people is always, and I mean *always*, more powerful than trying to "fix" or control them.

This is the way of God.

It is far more powerful to lead those you love with praise than with panic. Instead of assuming you know what someone needs to change, ask them. Learn to listen first and you will also learn deeper compassion and understanding for those around you. This is the place of real love: not compartmentalizing people into groups but allowing people to BE people.

Chapter 28

THE MAGIC OF "SOMETIMES"

I was coaching a client of mine once who is a single mother of two. She was telling me about how she "never" feels like she does "anything" right. If she is making dinner, her children are making a mess of the house. If she cleans the house, the children are sad that she isn't paying attention to them. And if she is playing with them, then the laundry never gets done.

She felt like a bad mom for all of the things she couldn't finish or perfectly do.

She said things like,

> "The laundry is *never* done."
> "My house is *always* a mess."
> "I *never* play with my kids enough. "
> "I'm *always* in a bad mood, and I hate it."
> "My kids never *seem* happy with me."

She was in tears as she was telling me this. It all seemed so true to her. *Of course it did.* It was her brain's pattern to put her in the all-or-nothing category to decide if she was a good or bad mom. *Either everyone is happy all the time, or I'm a bad mom. If the laundry is never done, I'm a mess.*

Her brain left out the truth. That's why she was in pain.

So I asked her, "Is it true that you *never* play with your kids?"

She said, **"No, I play with them a little everyday."**

I said, "Oh! Well isn't that good to know!"

Then I asked her, "Are you *always* in a bad mood?"

She said, **"Well no, just sometimes."**

I told her that *sometimes* **is where the magic is!**

Sometimes is where truth and peace live.

Have you ever met someone that is *always* or *never* anything? I haven't. I have only met people who are sometimes . . .

- sometimes happy,
- sometimes sad,
- sometimes stressed,
- sometimes relaxed,
- sometimes on time.

We now know that the brain lives in all-or-nothing. So from this moment on, every time you find yourself saying *never* or *always* about yourself or others, know that these are NOT truths.

Here are some examples of turning all-or-nothing thinking into something that is more likely true.

From, "My husband never cares how I feel,"
to
"My husband cares, but he may need more context before he understands."

From, "My kids never listen to me,"
to
"Sometimes my kids don't listen to me, but a lot of times they do."

From, "My house is always a mess"
to
"Parts of my house are messy, but a lot of it is clean."

Have you ever noticed how easy it is for us to give someone else grace for all of their imperfections, messes, mistakes, or flaws?

Like when you show up to a friend's house and hear her apologize for the mess—as she's worried about the dishes in the sink, the clothes on the floor, the crayon on the walls, and that she is not fully ready for the day—she probably thinks you are judging her and noticing everything that is out of place.

But really you just feel even more comfortable because you know your house looks the same. You don't think she is less of anything. You see how much she has on her plate, and you know the struggle because you live it too.

The mess, not the perfection, connects you.

You would probably tell her that you don't care if her house is a mess, you think she is doing an amazing job, and you love her the same.

It's so easy for us to give grace to others, but we often forget to give any to ourselves.

Imagine if you treated yourself like you treated your friend: not focusing on the mess but seeing all that she is taking on—all that she is trying to manage, all that is hard and overwhelming—and seeing all that she IS doing, not what she isn't; building her up, reminding her of all the good you notice, and telling her to not worry about needing it to look perfect.

If you talked to yourself this way, I promise you, you would break the cycle of depression and anxiety that runs on a loop.

Pause the judgmental thoughts, zoom out, and look at all you are taking on, what your intentions are, all that you ARE doing.

And give yourself **grace**.

If your brain is capable of giving grace to others then it is capable of giving it to you. You just have to direct that grace both inward and outward.

This isn't just a nice idea. This will change everything for you.

Grace is a Godlike love. It can accept a person even when they are imperfect. Grace is understanding that a person is more than what they do. Grace is forgiveness and love, even when it's messy.

When you're spiraling, try to zoom out to 30,000 feet—as if you were observing yourself and your life from the clouds. Notice all that you handle, the people you're helping, the heaviness in your heart, and the load you carry that no one sees. **And see it!** View yourself as you would view someone else, with no judgment, only deep compassion and understanding. I practice this at least once a day, especially when

I can only see what I'm not accomplishing and feel completely overwhelmed. I pause, zoom out, and take in the entire picture for a moment. This practice consistently brings relief and gratitude for everything I am striving to do and become.

I've witnessed countless clients transform their emotional lives by using this practice and embracing grace. This powerful mindset shifts you from a downward spiral of self-criticism to a state of relief and peace.

So be more kind to yourself through the mess, moods, sad days, overwhelm, AND ALL that you carry and try to make perfect.

Remember the "sometimes," and free yourself from the all-or-nothing thinking that has kept you in pain.

Section 7

RELATIONSHIPS

YOUR RELATIONSHIP WITH YOURSELF AFFECTS ALL OTHER RELATIONSHIPS.

Chapter 29

THE RELATIONSHIP
WITH YOURSELF

The foundation for healthy relationships *depends* on the degree to which we love and accept *ourselves*.

When we hold the belief that God's love must be earned, it influences our perception that all love—especially our own—requires earning.

Everyone I know and have worked with wants to improve the relationships in their lives. They all want to feel more connected with and loved by their spouse, sibling(s), mother, in-law(s), or friend(s). Relationships can bring the greatest joy and the deepest pain in this life. When we feel safe and loved in relationships, everything seems easier, and the opposite is also true. When our relationships are emotionally unsafe, disconnected, and painful, everything seems harder because most of our emotional human needs are dependent on healthy relationships.

Relationships have been important to both my life and work because I wholeheartedly believe that our primary purpose on this earth is to learn to love ourselves and others. Although it seems straightforward, it's one of the most challenging tasks due to the limitations of our minds.

Our brains focus on things that make loving difficult, like problems, mistakes, and imperfections. It is almost impossible to *feel* love when we focus on lack in ourselves and others.

Love and lack are opposites, just as love and condition are.

Because of this, love can seem hard to find, hard to keep, and hard for the human mind to trust, leading us to either chase it or run from it.

When we've been hurt in relationships, our brain associates love with pain, and it fears that by allowing ourselves to feel love, we risk losing it. If your brain has linked love to pain, it instinctively avoids love for self-protection and steers clear of vulnerability, closeness, and connection to avoid that familiar pain. Many people remain single not because they can't find someone but because they unconsciously sabotage relationships when they detect feelings of love, whether those feelings are *for* the other person or *from* them to someone else.

Love is never the danger.

It is the lack of love that hurts all of us.

And it's not the lack of love from others that creates emptiness; it's the lack of love for ourselves. When we focus on our faults and mistakes, constantly tearing ourselves down, it becomes nearly impossible to believe that someone else could truly love us.

The truth is, love doesn't really exist in conditions. We can conditionally accept ourselves and others, but true love cuts through all conditions.

This may not be a love you think you have experienced, and I get it. I had believed all love was conditional my whole life. And for us humans, maybe it often is. We make the conditions for accepting ourselves so high, so impossible to reach to ensure we never love ourselves. And then we wonder why we are sad, lonely, and depressed.

This is why! Because we don't like ourselves.

So many of us fear loving ourselves because we worry we won't seek improvement, we won't feel motivated to keep trying, and we won't catch ourselves when we do something wrong. We worry that if we like ourselves we will be lazy, we won't care and won't try. We have been conditioned to beat ourselves up believing it will make us be better, try harder, and stay motivated to improve.

The equations for love in our minds looks like this:

> The more I notice my flaws = the more I will fix them.
>
> The more I beat myself up = the better I will become.
>
> The more I resist love = the more love I will receive.
>
> The more I notice my imperfection = the more perfect I will be.

I have seen this my whole life, and I'm sure you have to.

How many times have you tried to criticize yourself into becoming a better version of yourself? How many times have you said something like,

> "I'm so stupid!"
> "What is wrong with me?!"
> "I'm the worst!"
> "I keep messing up"
> "No one will want me!"

and thinking that those words will be the kick in the pants you need to show up and be extra incredible the next day, only to find out that it doesn't get better, that the frustration you feel just makes everything feel awkward and hard causing you to once again fail at perfection?

It's like taking a bat and beating yourself up every time you get something wrong and thinking it will make you so excited to keep trying and fill you with confidence and energy.

Beating yourself up never helps. Never.

Throughout my years of coaching, I've heard hundreds of calls from women striving to be enough in their relationships—tirelessly trying to manage all the tasks, care for everyone, and maintain an image of perfection in both appearance and behavior.

And she is exhausted, frustrated, and lonely.

Her husband still doesn't seem satisfied with her efforts or her looks, and even if he is, she doubts it. Her kids still complain and don't listen. Her friends don't always invite her places, and her in-laws seem disappointed and judgy.

So she believes she isn't good enough for all of them.

But she doesn't notice the bully inside her head, The negative self-talk just feels so familiar. She is always wishing the people around her would change, be more kind and loving to her, tell her she is doing a good job, and be more appreciative of what she does.

She doesn't realize that she doesn't talk kindly or lovingly to herself; she doesn't tell herself good job or appreciate all she does either.

She desperately wants them to change so she can feel better, accepted, wanted, and valued because she doesn't accept or value herself.

And as long as she needs everyone else to change how they talk to her, change how they act around her, change how they perceive her— she will remain disempowered, disappointed, and resentful.

Some of the greatest harm we do to others stems from neglecting ourselves. When we don't take care of our needs, fill our own buckets, and create a sense of safety within ourselves, we start trying to fulfill these needs through other people. This makes us manipulative, needy, and controlling as we try to use others to replenish what we've depleted. This isn't love, it's abuse, and it is the very reason people often hurt each other in relationships. They haven't learned to take responsibility for their own emotional well-being. They don't know the importance of developing a healthy relationship within themselves first so they can have healthy connections with others.

When we fail to manage our emotions or create emotional safety for ourselves, we become selfish with those we claim to love. We fixate on changing them to meet our expectations. We try to control what they say and do so we can feel secure, needing them to be just what we want to fulfill our needs. No one can feel safe around us when we expect them to satisfy all our emotional needs.

An unhealthy relationship with yourself inevitably leads to unhealthy relationships with others. You'll find yourself at one end of the spectrum or the other: you'll either remain quiet and small, accepting avoidance, diminished respect, and abuse, or you'll become the one who tries to control, force, and manipulate the other.

To enjoy healthy, fulfilling relationships, we must first create a healthy relationship with ourselves. The brain doesn't know how to live simultaneously in self-hatred *and* have loving, healthy relationships with others.

It's time for women to learn how to turn this all around for themselves—

and realize that the most enticing, powerful and attractive thing you can do in any relationship is to

bring

your wholeness,

your authenticity,

your energy,

your ideas,

*the **you** that YOU like to be,*

not perfection.

Love doesn't need perfection. It doesn't care about that at all.

If you can bring the *you* that you already love into a relationship,

you ADD instead of deplete;
you give instead of take;
you want instead of NEED;
you love instead of resent;
you contribute instead of doubting yourself.

And unlike the tug-of-war we talked about earlier, you won't need to pull, convince, or prove that your spouse "should" love you. You drop the rope of desperation, and you allow them to **desire** you—who you are, what you offer, and the love that is enough for both of you.

How The Relationship with Self Impacts Athletes

I have coached many athletes over the years and this is the first thing we work on.

Athletes of all different ages and sports come to me when they feel stuck and are frustrated that they are not able to reach their goals despite practicing hard, eating right, doing what their coach says, and staying consistent.

As we dive into why they aren't improving, I ask them what they think about, how they talk to themselves, and how they feel when they mess up.

They almost always say,

> "Oh, I'm really hard on myself when I mess up."

> "I get mad at myself for not being able to do what I know I can do."

> "I focus on my mistakes, what went wrong, and get really frustrated with myself."

And I immediately understand why they are stuck and why improving feels so difficult. It's not because they can't improve. It's not because they don't know how. It's not because their body just isn't capable of reaching their goal.

It's only because they are thinking thoughts that generate

> frustration,

> anger,

> anxiety,

> defeat,

> disappointment.

241

When we feel those emotions our body slows down and becomes stiff and even frozen. Our energy plummets, and we go into fight-or-flight, which makes it really hard to do what we know how to do.

This is where most athletes end up if they have a pattern of self-hatred and perfectionism. What used to come naturally to them will feel hard. What was once fun will become dreadful. What used to feel exciting will fill them with pressure and anxiety.

And they will think something is wrong with them.

The truth is, nothing is wrong with them, their body, or their capability.

When you think something is wrong with you, your body simply believes it and *acts* like it.

This equation doesn't equal better results, yet most of us get stuck in this loop:

> The more frustrated I am with myself = the better I will play.

> The more I focus on what I did wrong = the better chance I have of getting it right.

We even try this equation with our spouse or children to get them to do what we want, criticizing or pointing out their flaws, hoping they will be better, only to find out they just feel discouraged and have no motivation to try.

Whenever I explain to my athletes that their self-perception significantly impacts their performance, they are surprised. They typically focus their attention on their physical training, diet, and the "how-tos of the sport" and overlook the power of their thoughts.

However, once they begin to shift their perception of themselves—focusing on what they believe they can achieve, why they're passionate about the sport, and what they truly love about it, while also learning to cheer themselves on, offer praise and encouragement, especially in moments of failure—everything changes! It consistently amazes them to discover the profound influence their self-beliefs have, leaving them stunned by the power they have over their emotions and their results.

I have seen athlete after athlete in many different sports transform their performance as they work with me. Most people assume this must be because I deeply understand each sport, know the strategies to winning, or maybe have excelled at these sports personally. And none of that is true. I did play sports growing up, but have never played the sports of most athletes I coach. I coach many track runners, and I have never run track. I never liked running and had never been to a track until a year ago.

I don't know all the hows, whats, and whens of each sport.

I just understand the brain and how thoughts affect the body.

I know how to help someone shift their mind from self-doubt, fear, and insecurity, to confidence, motivation, and belief!

I know how to help them tap into what they already know how to do and trust themselves.

I know how to help them feel empowered instead of anxious.

And with that, I know they can run faster, farther, stronger, and can play with more accuracy and power!

And it works every time!

Your results in life and all of your relationships depend on your relationship with yourself.

- Your performance in the game,
- the job you choose,
- the money you make,
- the boundaries you keep,
- the love you give and receive,
- what you allow in relationships, and
- what you choose to become

all depend on how you think and feel about yourself.

That is why *your* thoughts about you matter so much.

They create your reality, and impact all your relationships.

When you think over and over that you are enough, lovable, worthy, talented, and capable, you will not only believe it,

> **you will create healthy, fulfilling relationships.**
>
> **You won't accept abuse.**
>
> **You won't harm others.**
>
> **You will finally experience love.**

Chapter 30

POWERFUL COMMUNICATION FOR RELATIONSHIPS

I am so passionate about teaching women how to communicate in their relationships. Communication is an important piece to connection, safety, intimacy, parenting, and setting healthy boundaries in relationships.

First, I want you to think about your brain as the filter through which you are communicating. To reach someone's heart you have to go through their brain. And remember, the brain is using its experiences, insecurities, beliefs, and assumptions as the filter. So if your husband doesn't seem comfortable with communication, or quickly goes into fight-or-flight, you may not understand his filter.

The brain is looking for emotional and physical danger. If the brain has experienced negative emotion in conversations then it will be on guard for the next one.

If you and your husband find yourselves caught in a cycle of fighting, shutting down, saying things you don't mean, or leaving interactions feeling worse than when you started, your brain will begin to perceive communication as dangerous and seek to avoid it.

Brains don't want to walk into any potential negative emotion.

Here are 10 steps to creating more effective communication and reducing conflict.

1. **Talk to yourself first so you can have a good understanding of what you think and how you feel.** This will help create safety and regulate your nervous system before you enter the conversation.

    a. Ask yourself what you want to talk about with him, and *hear yourself out*. What do you want to say, and what are you hoping to hear from him?

    b. Ask yourself why this is important to you and what you are hoping to solve.

    c. Notice what solutions you already have.

    d. Allow yourself to have time and space to talk it through with yourself first without any response or reaction from anyone else.

2. **Ask yourself how you are feeling before this conversation and how you are hoping to feel after it.**

    a. If you are anxious, angry, or having any other negative emotion, see if you can move your body—take a quick walk, or take some deep, slow breaths—to bring down the intensity of the emotion.

    b. Allow yourself to feel and express this emotion with yourself without any judgment. This will help you feel centered and open.

3. **Trust yourself.**

    a. You know what you think, and you don't have to take on any thoughts or opinions that don't feel true to you.

    b. Remember that you don't need to be agreed with to trust what you know.

4. **You can only control your end of the conversation.**

    a. You don't need to control him; that is his job.

    b. If he says, "You don't know what you're talking about," "You're crazy," "You don't make any sense," or "I disagree," **it's OK.** You are still allowed to think and feel however you want.

    c. Remember, he can't take the truth from you, and you don't need him to agree for you to know what to do.

5. **Have clear boundaries before you start the conversation.**

    a. Something like this could be helpful: "I'd like to hear your ideas and opinions and hear what you have to say, but if you yell, swear, or try to fight, then I will leave the room."

    b. "I love you and want to hear what you have to say. If you fight with or avoid me, then I will make the decision I think is best."

6. **Start the conversation by putting the brain at ease.**

    a. Don't start with the same pattern that didn't work before. The brain quickly notices what feels familiar and it can shut down before you say much.

b. So, change the pattern. You can say something like, "Hey I'd like to hear your perspective on something. Let me know when you have a minute." Or try, "I'm trying to decide what I want to do about something, and I'd love your input."

c. But if you say "We need to talk," or use "you always" or "you never" sentences, the brain will quickly go into its pattern to protect itself.

7. **If your husband quickly goes to shame/blame, he may easily feel attacked in conversations, thinking he has done something wrong.**

a. If you notice your husband blaming you, saying his actions or feelings are your fault, just notice the shame blame loop he is in. *This is about him.* **This isn't about you.**

b. You don't need to convince him or argue about who's fault it is. Just breathe and ask yourself what is true here. Find it, and know it inside yourself.

c. Don't get into a battle over who's fault something is. Just bring the conversation back to what you are wanting to solve with him.

8. **You don't need him to agree with you for you to be right about your thoughts and opinions.**

a. If you think you need him to understand you *for you to understand you*, then you may become defeated quickly and shut down.

    b.   This is why the first steps are so important: understand yourself first, and know that you are safe even if he doesn't agree with your thoughts.

9. **If you want his opinion, ask for it, but know that you can take or leave it respectfully.**

10. **During the conversation, talk to yourself in your own mind to keep yourself regulated and safe.**

    a.   If he blames you, talk yourself through it in your mind.

    b.   If he says something you disagree with, let it stay with him.

    c.   You don't have to soak in every opinion and thought he offers. **They are his, so only take what is helpful for you to keep.**

It takes two people to fight, and if you're not one of them, there is no fight.

Your thoughts, opinions, and intuition are your own.

This doesn't mean you're always right.

You have a brain that doesn't think in facts, *and so does your husband.* The reason it can be hard to agree when we communicate is that we both think we are talking in facts, but facts are quite boring to the brain. Instead, the brain uses its own experience, assumptions, and guesses as the filter through which it understands things. So keep this in mind: *thoughts are just thoughts.* **You are allowed to take or leave any thought that doesn't resonate with you.**

If you can do these ten steps before you go into a conversation, your nervous system can stay regulated because it knows you will keep it safe. You aren't going in wide open and letting every thought or opinion be true for you or about you. This is how you can prevent yourself from shutting down or fighting.

I have done this for the last few years in my own marriage, and it has changed everything. We were never big fighters, but I would often give up and shut down if I didn't feel understood, agreed with, or safe. I didn't know how to handle being blamed when I didn't think it was my fault.

Now I can stay calm in almost any conversation because I take responsibility for my part and listen to him without feeling the need to agree with all his thoughts. His thoughts are his own, and by choosing to hear them, I can listen without worrying that everything he thinks is true or factual.

This guide empowers us as women to communicate with love and understanding for ourselves and those we love. When we feel secure, we can speak our truth, express our emotions openly, and listen without feeling threatened. We will be able to navigate our relationships more effectively, leading us to a greater sense of stability, feeling heard, and creating deeper connections.

Chapter 31

LOVE LANGUAGES

Love languages offer valuable insights into how you and others experience love. Throughout my years of studying the brain's behavior, I've developed my own simple theory about love languages.

As we discussed earlier, the brain doesn't solve for what it has enough of. It wants to solve problems, lack, and find what is missing. I believe a person's love language is the action they receive the *least*. And the way a person shows love is usually *the way they want to be loved*.

We give what we want to receive.

For example, if your husband expresses his love for you with physical touch often, it may feel good to you, but over time your brain won't need it as much, not because you don't want it but because you have enough of it, and that need is satisfied. But if your husband rarely buys you meaningful gifts or gives you words of affirmation, your brain will notice the lack and become more aware of and needy for it. Eventually, the physical touch won't feel like love to you as much as the rare gift or compliment.

You will crave what you lack:

- gifts if you don't receive gifts,
- quality time if people seem too busy for you,

- touch if you are often lonely and don't feel desired,
- words of affirmation if you don't receive enough praise,
- acts of service if you don't get the help you need or often feel like a burden for needing help.

Our childhood experiences significantly influence our love languages. For instance, if your parents showered you with wonderful gifts for birthdays and holidays but spent little quality time truly listening to and understanding you, you might highly value quality time and see it as love.

It's important to understand that if someone isn't expressing love in the way you need it most, it doesn't mean they don't love you.

Love is a personal emotion that is felt only by the individual experiencing it.

We are often told that other people "make" us feel loved, but no one can actually "make" you feel anything. We can't take the love we feel inside ourselves and hand it to another person, yet we all think this is the way love works.

We often argue and try to convince each other of love in relationships, second-guessing it all the time, making all their actions "mean" they love us or don't love us. This becomes an exhausting game for everyone and often leads to break-ups, strained relationships, or divorce.

We either get tired of trying to convince someone we love them, or we constantly fear the other person doesn't love us back. And because we can never know exactly how someone else feels, we are left to guess. This leaves us looking for all the ways love is lacking instead of noticing it in abundance.

I think it's really helpful to tell your spouse how you feel most loved and ask them how they feel it too. Then, make an effort to show love in the way that means the most to them.

But keep in mind that your spouse will often show love in the way that resonates most with them, and even if it's not how you prefer, their love is still there. Likewise, you likely express love in the way that feels most natural to you.

Love can't be measured, and we can't feel someone's love for us. Only they can feel their love for you. Your job is to allow yourself to be loved, to believe love is there even when it's presented imperfectly.

When you allow yourself to believe you are loved, you will be able to *feel love. You allow it in,*

and it's yours to keep.

Chapter 32

RECOGNIZING ABUSIVE PATTERNS AND CREATING BOUNDARIES

Throughout history, humans have developed patterns of thought, behavior, and beliefs that have been passed down through generations. Women, in particular, have inherited patterns dictating what they must do and be to get their needs met. For centuries, women depended on men for basic human essentials—food, shelter, and safety—sacrificing much of their freedom, voice, opinions, and desires to remain sheltered and alive. They were subjected to arranged marriages and silenced from speaking, preaching, or leading.

The world has shifted and changed so much for women in a short time. We live in a very different type of world now than women did even fifty years ago. But if we aren't careful, we will carry those old beliefs and patterns with us today.

When women don't have clarity and certainty on who they are and believe they need a relationship to feel fulfilled and whole, they will allow unacceptable behavior in their relationship. **When women still believe they need a man to be whole or valuable, they will accept almost any man.**

Men can sense this in women, especially if they are looking for it. They can tell if you crave their attention and lack confidence in your own worthiness or respect. They sense the desperation, and they will often test boundaries to see what they can get away with. Their brain wants to know how much effort is required to get what it wants. **This is what brains do.**

Abusive men are looking for insecurity, neediness, and desperation in a woman, even if those men don't realize that about themselves. If they think they can have you for simple sweet words and a nice gesture every now and then, they will give the amount needed to keep you, but not more. Their brain, just like yours, wants to conserve its energy. If you will stay with them, make them food, take care of them, forgive them endlessly, be what they need no matter how they treat you in return, their brain learns how little energy it needs to expend to keep you, and it doesn't want to do more than what is required to have its needs met.

There's usually no amount of begging them to give you more that will work long-term. You can ask, cry, beg, but his brain knows. He knows your boundaries. He knows that you will stay because you have always stayed no matter what.

Many women navigate the demands of childcare, housework, and often a job, all while dealing with an abusive spouse. Their husbands expect to come home to dinner on the table, a spotless house, cheerful children, and everything perfectly organized. Clothes for the next day are expected to be washed and ready. These men judge their wives' success by the smooth running of the household, overlooking the constant undoing of her efforts by little hands throughout the day.

Asking an abusive man for more time or energy when you have always stayed without it is like asking a toddler to clean up the kitchen and do the dishes before they get a snack when they've never had to do so before. If you've always done it for them and made it easy, never requiring such things, they aren't going to immediately do something hard for the reward they have always received without effort.

Brains learn patterns. This is what they are good at. This kind of man figures out the amount of energy required to keep you, learning that if he needs to give some apologies here and there, or tell you that you are beautiful for you to melt and just keep going, he will.

Words don't expend much human energy, so it's usually the thing the brain will go to first to get what it needs. Words mean more when we feel the genuineness and when they match up with action.

Words with action equals trust.

So, if you are only getting nice words and rinse-and-repeat apologies, **it's time to change the pattern. And the way to change the pattern is to set and enforce boundaries.**

Boundaries

Healthy boundaries are rooted in love—love for yourself and for the other person. They aren't about control, as we can't dictate others' actions. Everyone has the right to choose their own behavior and responses.

A boundary communicates clearly what behavior is and isn't acceptable to you, serving as a guideline for respecting your personal space and emotional well-being. It helps others understand your limits and creates mutual respect in relationships.

Healthy boundaries aren't meant to push people away or end the relationship. Boundaries help you keep the relationships you desire to keep while keeping yourself safe and protected along the way.

Boundaries don't tell people what they can and can't do; they tell the other person what you will and will not accept, what **you will do** if they choose a behavior that crosses your boundary.

For example, if your spouse is an alcoholic and drives your kids while he is intoxicated, and you don't want your kids to be in that situation, you could set a boundary like this:

"I don't want you driving the kids while you are drunk, so if you choose to take them somewhere while you are drinking, I will call the cops every single time because their safety is my top priority."

Notice how you are not telling them what they can and can't do; you are telling them what you will do for yourself (and your children) with what they choose.

If you have a boundary about how others speak to you, like not wanting to be sworn at or disrespected in conversations, you might say, "I don't want to be sworn at, called names, or disrespected, so if that happens, I will leave the room or hang up the phone."

A boundary doesn't dictate their behavior; it simply expresses what you will and won't tolerate, respecting both them and yourself. It also clearly communicates what actions you will take if that behavior occurs.

For a boundary to hold, you have to keep your end of it consistently. Otherwise, their brain will learn that you don't really mean it, and they will take advantage of your leniency.

If you are in a relationship where your intuition says, "This is not right," or the relationship is abusive in any way, trust yourself.

This is why God gave you feelings, so you can have a knowing of what is right and wrong for you to help you make powerful decisions with certainty.

I coach many women who are in toxic relationships, and they feel like they have to stay because of their children, or money, or fear that their spouse will be an awful ex. Or because they don't think they can do it alone.

Relationships are so personal, so don't try to get permission or advice from friends or family, but definitely seek support and safe spaces to express yourself.

If you are going to leave an abusive relationship, I invite you to receive the answer to do so for yourself. No one can perfectly know your experience and what is going on for you in your relationship. And you are always allowed to find that answer within yourself. You don't need permission to leave any relationship that is hurting you. And you definitely don't need your partner's permission.

No one owns anyone in relationships.

It is an agreement, and if at any time you don't feel safe, or you want to leave for reasons that make sense to you, **that is yours to choose.**

You deserve to be loved, seen, and treated well in a partnership. Don't settle for less because you fear you're not enough for something better.

Section 8

YOU ARE MORE THAN ENOUGH

EMBRACE YOUR DIVINITY, KNOWING YOU ARE MORE THAN ENOUGH TO CREATE AND SHAPE YOUR LIFE IN THE WAY YOU DESIRE.

Chapter 33

THE UNSEEN BRILLIANCE
OF MOTHERHOOD

As a mother, your job is unlike most because in the workplace, adults work with other adults. They collaborate as a team, delegate tasks, and solve problems together. They have the luxury of using the bathroom in privacy, eating whenever they're hungry, and setting boundaries. And the best part? They get paid for all their efforts!

Mothers don't have this at home. There is no efficient delegating, no teamwork, no one coming to help or strategize for how to accomplish all the tasks of the day.

Instead, she has little people undoing every piece of laundry she folds, spilling juice on the floor she just mopped, squeezing out the toothpaste she just bought, peeing on the floor she just cleaned, dumping every crayon and marker out just to find the right one, all while asking her a million questions about how the world works, followed with 10,000 whys with every answer she gives—all while she is trying to keep the toddlers out of the knives and the neighbor friends from waking the baby, making sure everyone is fed, and then cleaning it all up again.

Nothing stays done, no one stops moving and needing. There is no strategy that sticks, no other adult to share the load, no sitting, no quiet time to use her brain.

Let's not forget that brains crave rewards. Every kind of job is incentivized by a reward, otherwise no one would do it. If you take a minute to think about what reward a mother gets at the end of the day or week of more than full time, 24-7 work, what is it? What does she have to look forward to?

A big paycheck? A congratulations? A thank you? A gift? Mom of the Month award?

Nope. None of that.

Just everyone wanting more.

How remarkable is that? How absolutely incredible is it that mothers do this? They do a job that no one can afford and no one would sign up for.

So remember how capable you are, how much you can handle, and how smart and resilient you are.

This type of constant work is so difficult for the human brain, a brain that wants to conserve energy and receive rewards for doing hard things. Women push through all of that. They have an insane, Godlike ability to work, create, care for, and love without reward.

And it will forever blow my mind.

When I sit with women, I often hear them say that

> they aren't enough for the people they love;
> they can't keep the house clean enough;

they don't always make fresh, homemade meals three times
a day;
they are overweight and don't exercise enough;
they lost their patience with their children;
the closets aren't organized;
they didn't plan the most epic birthday party for their two-
year-old;
they forgot to take the sick neighbor a meal;
they haven't cleaned out the fridge;
they didn't go to bed early enough;
they ate too many calories;
they haven't started a business or made any money;
their husband isn't satisfied, and they wish they could stop
disappointing him;
they don't have good ideas;
they don't know how to be a good mom;
they aren't pretty enough,

> skinny enough,
> healthy enough,
> smart enough,
> organized enough—

just not enough of the wanted things,

and too much of the unwanted things.

I call BS.

And say NO!

No more of this!

Put down the bat, my friends. No more beating ourselves up. No more focusing on made-up ideals of what a woman "should" be, what she should get done in a day, or how she should look and feel.

Stop.

You are a human being, not a robot. If your husband wants to marry a robot, **let him.**

But until then, he married a human who has birthed other humans, all of whom are brilliant and miraculous, all of whom come with different skills and emotions.

It's part of the magic.

You are not a human doing, you are a human being.

Being is enough. All the stuff you do is just the icing on the cake!

If your husband doesn't value you or notice what you do, it doesn't mean *you* can't notice and value what you do. What you value about you is more important, and if you value all you do and all you are **it won't matter if he does.**

We can't control what he notices, what matters to him, or what he thinks is successful.

It's not actually his to decide.

No more of this not-enoughness.

You are and do more than enough.

Period.

End of story.

If your husband wants the house to be cleaner, he can clean it too. Weird how that works, right? If he likes his clothes to be cleaned a certain way, he can clean them too.

I don't say this with animosity. It's just the truth. He can create what matters to him, just like you can. If it's more important to you that you took the kids to the park, gave them baths, fed them, and kept them alive than it is for the house to be perfectly clean,

own that.

Your priorities are yours. They are yours for a reason. Trust that what matters to you, and how you choose to raise your children and take care of what is important to you, is your choice. And it is good *as it is*.

Your children came to you. You are the mom for them.

Your way, personality, unique gifts, and strengths are what they need.

They don't need two parents that think the same way.

They need the YOU that you are.

Chapter 34

OWNING YOUR UNIQUE
IMPACT IN MARRIAGE

When women believe God to be a Father only, they see themselves as only daughters, not as ultimate creators, leaders, and Gods in the making. As a coach, I see this often in the women I work with. It's the blind spot that keeps women stuck, small, and unsure of who they are.

So often when I am working with women on their business ideas, parenting, relationships, intimacy, dreams, and goals, they will say things like:

> "I would create a business, but my husband won't let me."

> "I want to discipline my child this way, but my husband doesn't agree."

> "I would love to travel to this place, but my husband doesn't like to travel."

> "I told my husband about my business idea, but he doesn't think it's worth the money."

> "I struggle with intimacy, but I don't want to say anything to make my husband upset or think I don't love him."

266

It's like these women don't even realize that they can't make a decision for themselves without permission or approval from their husbands. And I'm not saying they shouldn't communicate, come together, discuss topics, and hear each other's perspectives and ideas. I think that is crucial in relationships.

But the woman often sees her husband as the ultimate decision-maker, the one who has the final say. So she tiptoes up to him and tries to convince him of something she wants

like a child to a parent.

And if he says no, she thinks that's the end of it. Or she sneaks around him, hiding the thing she wants to do—stashing money, pulling tags off new clothes, hopping out of bed if he notices she slept in—all so she doesn't get in trouble.

To keep the peace, she lets him be right and rarely voices disagreement. She changes out of her sweats before he gets home and stresses about having dinner ready upon his arrival. She frequently apologizes for his discomfort and constantly strives to meet his expectations.

The list goes on and on.

For the longest time I couldn't figure out why. And then one day it hit me:

Women don't know WHO they are!

They have picked up patterns from previous generations when women weren't allowed the same freedoms we now have, when women didn't dare step out of line for fear they would be rejected or left for someone better, when women were supposed to be seen but not heard. Countless fears and patterns have been passed down, shaping the perceptions that little girls form as they grow.

They watched their moms ask, plead, and hide.

And so they thought that is what they were supposed to do as well,

> *as if keeping husbands happy was what women were made for.*

I wonder who came up with that idea? **Probably not a woman.**

I see the fear in my clients' eyes when they think their husbands are unhappy with them in any way. They almost can't think of anything else but trying to please him again.

I know this fear runs deep and feels so real.

I grew up hearing many stories about men who left their wives—men that met someone at work, fell in love, and abandoned their families, leaving a wake of trauma for their posterity. This is the story of many of my own ancestors.

And I know this is not an unusual story.

Almost every woman has likely heard the heartbreaking story of a single mother whose husband left for someone else. Throughout history, such stories are sadly all too common, but especially today.

With pornography on every screen, so accessible and easy to hide, men don't have to create a relationship with someone in person anymore. They aren't required to dress up, be on their best behavior, pick her up for a date, cover the dinner bill, listen attentively, treat her well, and hope she enjoys their company. They can avoid being vulnerable or rejected. They don't have to leave the comfort of their home or couch anymore. They have a whole world of options at their fingertips, right there in their pocket all day long.

I've sat with so many women deeply shaken by this kind of pain. I listen as they speak through tears, questioning themselves, wondering what is wrong with them, asking why they aren't enough to keep their husband's interest and attention, wrestling with feelings of deep betrayal.

Pornography can feel like a tidal wave ever-growing in the distance, one that's impossible to stop or escape. Many are trying to find refuge, desperate to keep their husbands from it, trying to keep his attention, checking his devices, constantly worried they are being compared to a photoshopped girl on the internet.

And yet the wave grows bigger and bigger with more ways to access pornography and more ways to hide it.

I've sat with countless women who have just discovered that their husbands have been addicted to pornography throughout their entire marriage.

Many women share stories of feeling undervalued in their relationships, exemplified by experiences such as this: a mother living in mustard stained sweats, nursing a newborn five times a night, discovers that her husband has been looking at other women—women who haven't given birth to his children; women who don't spend nights caring for sick kids, changing wet sheets, wiping away tears, or rocking babies to sleep; women who are ten or twenty years younger, with airbrushed bodies meticulously photoshopped into society's ideal image of what a wife *should* look like—

and it devastates her.

For she has given her body to create life. She has given her rest to hold children in the night. She has given her mind to resolve tantrums, make lists, and find everyone's matching socks. She has given her energy to the life and well-being of her children so they could carry *her husband's last name*.

Discovering that he was drawn to women who never made such sacrifices for him, women who don't even know his name, nor he theirs. The attention this mother desperately seeks and needs is being given to a nameless, often faceless person on the internet, while she feels drained by the countless family demands, no longer recognizing herself in the mirror.

This woman needs support, desires to be seen, loved, and wanted through all of this.

Pornography steals the time and attention of her husband. He gets a break from stress, a break from hard, and some added pleasure and dopamine, all while she takes care of everyone's needs but her own while waiting for him to acknowledge her. And why would he when she will do all of this without his attention?

Even with their hearts shattered in pieces, women show up.

They show up fueled by love

> because they ARE LOVE.
> It is built into their DNA.

That is the absolute Godlike power and love that is in women.

They do work no one pays for, not because it isn't valuable but because *it is*.

THE MOST VALUABLE.

And no one can afford it.

It is the very work of God.

God creates mountains, oceans, stars, and galaxies—all things the human mind cannot create, all things our minds can't figure out.

And so do women.

Women create life without thought,

> *without knowing how.*

And no one comprehends how it's done. **It is completely miraculous.**

Women do the work of miracles.

And they do it without pay or praise

> **because so does God.**

God breathes life into everything without our noticing it, without our asking for it, without our praise or pay. We just trust every day that we will wake up and be taken care of. We will have the perfect amount of air to breathe, gravity to hold us, sun to warm our faces, light to see, food to eat.

A mother—a Divine Mother—takes care of all these things as you sleep, just as you take care of these things for your children as they sleep: making sure they have food when they wake up, clothes to wear, crayons to color with, activities, school, friends, and birthday parties.

The work of a mother:

> **she is in you and you in Her,**
> doing the unnoticed work of God—of life and of creation.

The work you do as a woman, as a mother, can't be bought, for it is too holy.

The human mind can't comprehend all that a woman can do.

No man would sign up for it, and no man could do it.

Think of a man trying to push an eight-pound baby through his most tender area. How do you imagine that would go? How many children do you think would make it to earth?

One. Just one.

Own this power that you have because it is yours. Nothing about you is less than, weak, or not enough.

And anytime you believe you are not enough, **know that it is a lie.**

If your husband doesn't agree with your ideas, that is OK. Let him disagree. Don't argue or prove. Just breathe, and remember, he doesn't know how he even came to be. He doesn't know everything. He isn't supposed to know what you know. It isn't always going to make sense to him, and that's OK! Try explaining pregnancy and birth to him and see if he thinks it sounds like a good idea.

When you leave him in charge of all that you do for a day, what happens? Does he think of all the things you do? Does he remember to take care of all the things you do? Does he multitask while making sure there is order and beauty throughout the house? Is he making dinner, signing kids up for soccer, arranging for someone to pick up the kids from school, nursing a baby with one arm and stirring the pot with the other while telling the older kid how to spell the word "elephant"?

Or does it look like he just kept them alive?

And we love that he kept them alive.

But notice.

You have different brains, different gifts, different ideas and capabilities. You function differently, you see things differently.

You are supposed to.

Don't view your husband as a point of comparison, as the source of all your answers or as the one to grant you permission.

If we did that, we would just have two of him. And we only need one!

The world needs women to be what they were sent here to be—to own their gifts, to see their differences as their magic and their ideas as Godliness.

You are not supposed to think like your husband, *or you would.* You are not supposed to function like him, *or you would.*

It is the balance of the two that creates the most magic. And if you don't fully show up in yours, it will be off balance. We need women to show up unafraid of what they bring to the table, to speak with conviction, to trust themselves and know when to lead.

You are already kind and loving. You already care how everyone feels. That won't go away if you show up in your wisdom.

Believe that you have so much to offer and that if you feel passionately or strongly about something, **it's yours to do, it's yours to create**

without permission or acceptance.

Chapter 35

YOUR BELIEF IS YOUR POWER

In my coaching practice, I listen to countless women share their frustrations, grief, exhaustion, feelings of overwhelm and anxiety. I sit with them as they cry, and then watch as they quickly wipe away their tears, embarrassed by the belief that they "shouldn't cry" and "have nothing to cry about."

I hear them say,

> "Sorry. I don't know why I'm crying. It's so stupid."
> "I should be stronger."
> "I'm such a crybaby."
> "I hate when I cry."
> "I should be grateful."
> "It could be worse."
> "I'm just a mess."
> "Something is wrong with me."

I hear them.

And sometimes I cry with them because the pain is familiar.

We are asked to carry the burdens of the world—with a smile, never allowing our emotions to be seen because if we do, we are perceived as weak or ungrateful.

Women often don't have a safe space where they can communicate their thoughts and feelings without judgment or being told to look at the bright side.

In relationships, women often take on the mother or child role:

> taking care of him like a mother and then resenting him,
> or acting like his child—needing permission or approval and
> feeling afraid.

I believe one underlying reason for this mindset among women globally is the absence of a feminine representation in Heaven. Our language lacks a feminine term for God, leaving many women to wonder . . .

> *am I Divine— Godly, wise and glorious—*
> *or do I remain in the background doing the*
> *unpaid, unnoticed work without mention or praise,*
> *taking on the role of creation, and then fading away into the*
> *background?*

Men get to imagine being a God someday: all-powerful, all-knowing, worshipped, and loved.

Women imagine meeting God as a child to a Father, but not becoming Him. They know they won't be a God the Father someday, but their husband will be. They have no view or language telling them what role they will take on in Heaven, no divine prototype that matches their feminine being.

And because of this image, young girls and women have thought they just aren't enough to be a God—to be worshipped, praised, or prayed to.

I believe many of us aren't consciously aware of this, and some might not think it even matters. However, through my years of studying psychology and coaching women, I've realized that it does matter. This lack of a divine feminine prototype influences us subconsciously, residing deep beneath the surface for women of diverse faiths and backgrounds.

Women often feel confused about why they don't fully feel equal, why they feel so vulnerable in their marriage, why they worry over the smallest details that their husband doesn't seem to stress over. Why does he seem to be so comfortable with messes or mistakes, but she can't be? Why can he relax at home while she attaches her value to all of it?

She worries that she could be easily replaced by another woman who might do everything better and bring him more happiness, yet he remains satisfied with himself just as he is.

Men are conditioned to *want*, and women are conditioned to *be wanted*,

causing men to feel deserving of their wants, while women feel undeserving of theirs.

And maybe this is why: it's like the undertow we cannot see, the one we don't speak of because no one has a satisfying answer.

Given the traditional view of God, men may struggle to perceive their wives as equally worthy, holy, or divine since women are rarely spoken of in such a way. This perspective can hinder a man's ability to recognize his wife as someone with power and authority or as someone he doesn't feel good enough for. It challenges his ability to see her as someone whom the world reveres and looks to for answers, truth, or guidance.

I don't believe that one gender is better than the other. Both are divine, both are needed, both are creators and Gods in the making. But one has been left out of this role in all our worship and language.

It has an impact that we may never fully realize or be able to measure. And to reiterate, *I didn't want to be the one to write about it*. I don't like breaking the social norms. I don't like speaking about what no one wants to talk about. Nothing makes me more uncomfortable.

But this message has burned within me since I was young, when it pushed me to compete with the boys at recess. I constantly felt the need to prove that I was equal, just as valuable and capable of anything they could do—almost as if they were promised a special place in Heaven that I heard was beyond my reach.

And my brain, just like any brain, wanted to solve for the lack, wanted to understand the void and fill it.

When I decided to write a book, I had a deep knowing it might be this one, and I told God no! Every time this message rose within me, I feared it. And I would ask God to give me a different message to write.

> *Give me something that feels comfortable to everyone.*
>
> *Give me something we can all agree on, something that doesn't rock the boat or feel weird, even something intriguing, fun, or fictional.*
>
> *But not this.*

I wrestled with God for months before I left for this book-writing adventure. I knew I needed to write something, but I wanted *this* message to come through someone else,

> *not me.*

As I closed my eyes and surrendered to what I was here to write, this whole book flowed through my hands in a matter of hours.

Hours!

Not weeks.
Not months or years, like most books.

Minutes and hours is all it took for over 50,000 words to land on these pages. I still can't comprehend it. That doesn't seem possible, especially not for me.

So maybe this message isn't for everyone. And if it doesn't land for you, that is OK! Take what fits, and leave what doesn't, as always.

But if it's for you, then let it fill you with hope and a love that maybe you've never considered was yours before.

You are not just a girl, just a woman, or just a mom.

You are everything.

I know many women feel like they exist solely for others, feeling like *just* a caregiver who ensures everyone else believes in themselves. They're not the ones who lead, speak up, say no, or prioritize self-care. They are never paid, never desired, never enough.

Maybe *you think that it only matters what other people think of you,* and that if you can *get people to love you, praise you, compliment you,* **you will be saved from your internal anguish and self-doubt.**

I know *the answers and the love you seek feel like they are outside of you.*

I know *you wish and pray that someone will come and just love you enough for you to believe you are worthy and valuable.*

The truth is, the love you desire is not outside of you.

The pain that you live in was built by the beliefs of your own mind:

- the rules you gave to yourself,
- the way you talk to yourself,
- the love you are never willing to give *to you,*
- the grace you withhold,
- how you beat yourself up for every flaw or mistake,
- the doubt you carry around rehearsing and believing.

This is your cage and your pain.

This is why you accept abuse, why you accept less from others and from yourself.

You don't believe you deserve more.

Your belief is your power. When you change your belief, you change the rules you live by. You expand your own walls when you allow yourself to be loved BY YOU.

Magic Wand

Imagine I waved a magic wand and dispelled all your self-doubt, every single "not good enough" thought and sentence you've ever believed. What if I could make you forget all the times you've stood in front of the mirror and counted your flaws, wanting to be different in 100 ways; all the times you've scrolled through social media wishing you lived someone else's life; all the words you've heard growing up from parents, teachers, and friends who questioned who you are?

What if I waved my wand and they were all gone?

Clean, cleared out.

And you were open again: open to what is possible for you, open to new ideas about who you are, open to love, and excited for all you were going to create.

And with the flick of my wand you were allowed to believe anything you wanted.

Imagine you believed you were *more than good enough* for anyone or anything.

Imagine that you actually believed The Divine Mother and Father—together—created you with such purpose, such care, and that you are like Them.

They breathe with you, walk with you, and believe in you.

You are a God in the making.

You are already enough. Your desires are already divine, and you can't mess anything up.

Imagine if you allowed yourself to be so loved that it didn't matter who else loved you.

Imagine you were so filled with unconditional love that it spilled over onto everyone else with ease.

What if everywhere you went you believed everyone loved you **because all you knew was love from yourself?**

Imagine you weren't looking for love or worried that you might get hurt or lose love because you believe love can't be lost.

Imagine you loved your life as God loves your life, that you loved your ideas, your body, your dreams with such reckless abandon that limits could no longer exist.

And others are drawn to your light, wondering how you dare to live without walls, restrictions, or limits. You create every day believing you are worth the time, energy, and space with zero guilt and with no shame.

What if you gave space and time for your every dream and desire because that matters to you?

And imagine if being good enough no longer mattered because you are good enough for you, never lacking, never doubting.

You have you, and that is always enough.

If you believed this, what would change from how your life is now?

Record your thoughts here.

_____

_____

_____

_____

_____

_____

_____

If you want to be this version of you, all you have to do is change the old belief.

Start by questioning it, then find the mistruths and answer them with the truth of who you know you are and who you want to be.

Rinse and repeat until your brain drops the old and believes the new.

And watch your life change in ways you never thought possible, as I've seen countless clients and myself transform through this practice.

Chapter 36

YOU ARE LOVE

Love is not something you have to chase,
And no one can give it to you.
Love is who you are.

When a baby is born, do we hold her for the first time and notice all she's not?

Imagine holding your newborn for the first time, minutes after she was born, and thinking, *hmm, she weighs too much. Where are her abs? Her legs are too short, she doesn't have enough hair, and her eye color isn't right. She's just not enough for me to love her.*

We never say that about a newborn baby.

I find it so interesting. It's almost the only time our brains don't see someone as not good enough, even though babies **don't do anything for us**.

Your baby can't walk, talk, feed herself, clean the house, or help with chores. She doesn't make money or have an airbrushed body. She just lies there, breathes, cries, and needs.

And somehow our brains think she is more than enough! Perfect even! We think she is beautiful and worth every sacrifice it took to bring her to earth. She doesn't make anything *easier,* and yet, we are all delighted! Fascinated with each breath and sound she makes! If she blinks her eyes, we all cheer in awe and wonder!

She didn't have to earn our love. She *couldn't earn it.* All she does is take and need. That baby *does* nothing for anyone. And yet, the love we have is beyond comprehension.

How can that be?

It is because we see her and love her as God does.

It's a love that doesn't *need* anything—a selfless love, a perfect love—a love that transcends the human mind, rules, and beliefs.

It's a love that takes our breath away, a love that fills the room and touches everyone that enters that space.

What if we loved people the way we love newborn babies, no matter their age or what they do? We are just in complete awe of them like we are with babies—oohing and awing over them—seeing all they ARE instead of all they are not, seeing the beautiful features on their faces, grateful for their life and breath, in complete wonder of their existence and uniqueness.

We do not need to fix or control them, nor put them in categories or boxes, but we see them as the miracles they are, believing they are worth all the effort we pour into them when they are needy and difficult. Even when we are tired, and all they do is make a mess and cry, we love them.

I **now** believe that is how God loves us—how our Divine Mother and Father love us.

They are watching us here in awe and wonder, cheering for everything we learn for the first time, picking us up when we fall, holding us when we cry, protecting us from danger, ever watching, ever loving—not needing or fixing—just grateful for our every breath.

Babies can teach us a very important lesson on love, the most important message of all being **that love is not something we earn, it is for all without condition.**

Love makes no demands and is not scarce. Love is the most abundant thing there is! For no service is given without love as the fuel. No sacrifice is made without love driving it. Love is the very vibration that keeps everything alive.

Love is the *why*!

Why we create life, why we sacrifice for it, why we selflessly go into battle to save lives unmet. Love is the reason we do any of it. It's why we do jobs we don't like, wake up in the night to care for sick kids, and go without so others can have more.

Love is the reason behind it all!

If love had to be earned, we would never love a newborn baby. It wouldn't make sense. Babies don't give us anything or make anything easier for us. They come here and make everything harder. And somehow we just can't help but love them more than anything else.

Why?

Because it is Godlike love.

I didn't always believe this. I tried to earn love my whole life, thinking there was never enough of it for me, or I wasn't enough for it. I thought everyone had to earn it, and there was only enough for the best people, the ones doing it right—the ones that didn't miss church, the ones that read, prayed, and checked the attendance roll. I thought they had earned God's love more than others. And so I tried to do all of those things perfectly too. I didn't believe I was loved like a newborn baby is loved—just for living, breathing, and trying.

I met people of all different cultures, religions, beliefs, and I saw goodness. I felt love. I stood in wonder of who they were. I heard their ideas, coached them on their creations, and sat with them in their grief. I cried with them through their pain and cheered for their accomplishments. And I realized it didn't matter what they thought, believed, or did.

I loved them.

And as a mother, I felt the only unconditional love I've ever known, the kind of love without rule or condition. And my children love to test this love. They often say, "Mom, would you still love me if I did this or that?"

And the answer is and will always be, "Yes!"

That same love is *in* all of us and *for* all of us.

It's the love of a mother staring at her newborn baby and not *needing* anything from her baby.

Love is all around us, within everyone, and through everything. It's the very essence of life, the vibration that sustains us, and the substance of heaven. It's the feeling we long for above all else. You don't have to earn it, prove yourself worthy of it, or follow any rules to receive it.

And just like a newborn baby, you are loved just because you exist.

My hope is that knowing this will give you rest, lift the pressure, unravel the perfectionism, ease the burden, and calm the rush of trying to chase imaginary enoughness, as if you must reach it to be perfectly loved.

You are **already** there, all you need to do is *believe* it now.

For you are divine.

www.ingramcontent.com/pod-product-compliance
Lightning Source LLC
Chambersburg PA
CBHW021218130626
46554CB00004B/1270